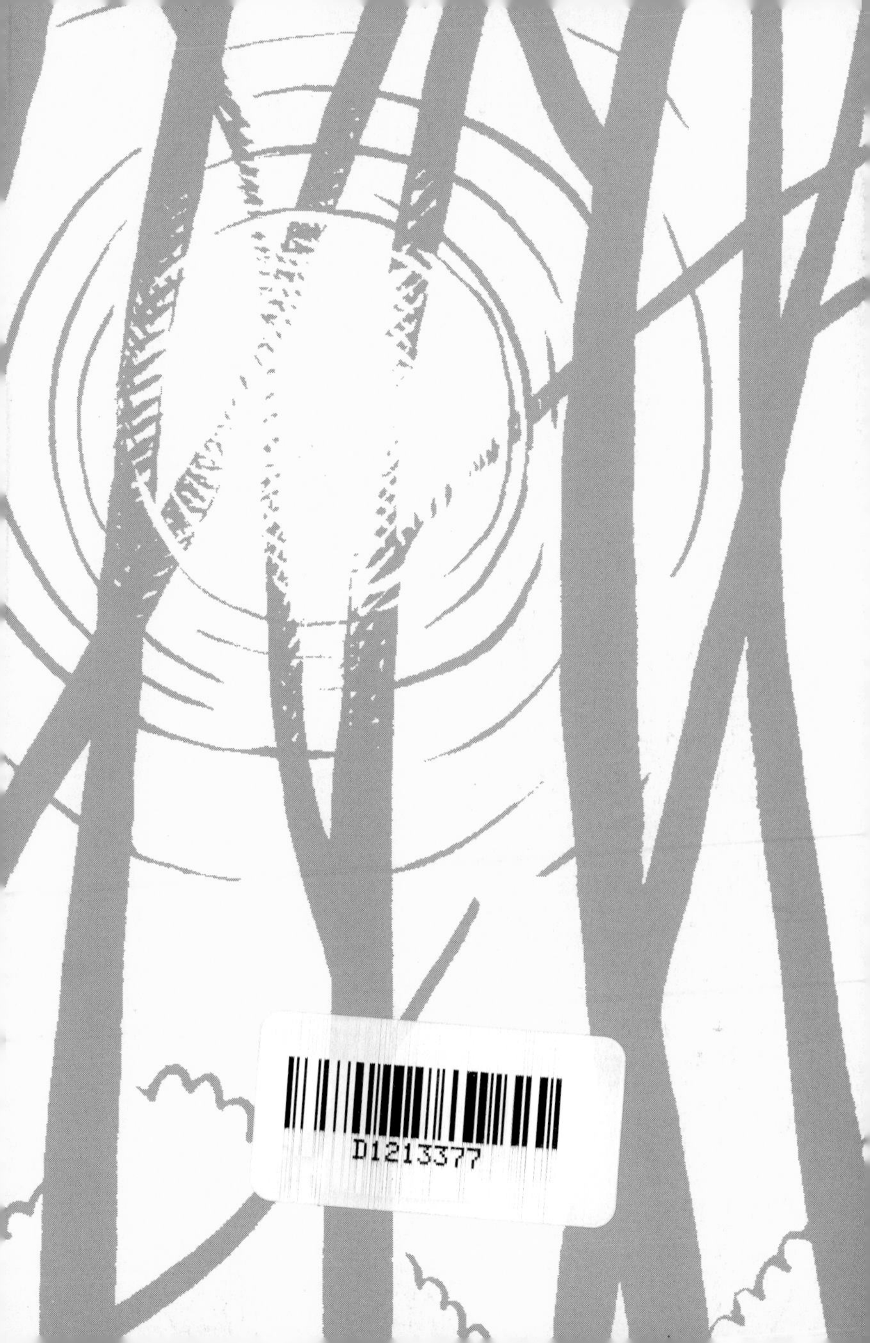

Pulpatoon Pilgrimage
Published by AdHouse Books
Copyright: Joel Priddy 2002

isbn 0-9721794-0-2
10 9 8 7 6 5 4 3 2 1

"Dondé habite el olvido"
by Luis Cernuda.

Design: Chris Pitzer
pitzer@adhousebooks.com

AdHouse Books
1224 Greycourt Ave.
Richmond, VA 23227-4042
www.adhousebooks.com

First Printing, 2002
Printed in Canada by Quebecor.

"Pulpatoon" is a medieval
word for a savory pie of
pressed meat or vegetables.
It has nothing to do with
comics, or old magazines,
or even this story. But it
sounds neat, doesn't it?

# Pulpatoon
## pilgrimagE

THIS BOOK
* IS A GIFT FROM *

ART BY KALI CIESEMIER

THE
* SMALL PRESS EXPO *
WWW.SPXPO.COM / SPX.TUMBLR.COM

Thanks to Kim, who, back in the day,
encouraged and cajoled me
when I needed it most.

And many thanks to Chris Pitzer
for wrapping my pig in such a pretty poke.
**- Joel Priddy**


Thanks to Kelly Alder, Ted Adams &
Jeff Mason for your help in getting it going.
Thanks to Joel for letting me play in his sandbox.
And thanks to Lisa.
**- Chris Pitzer**

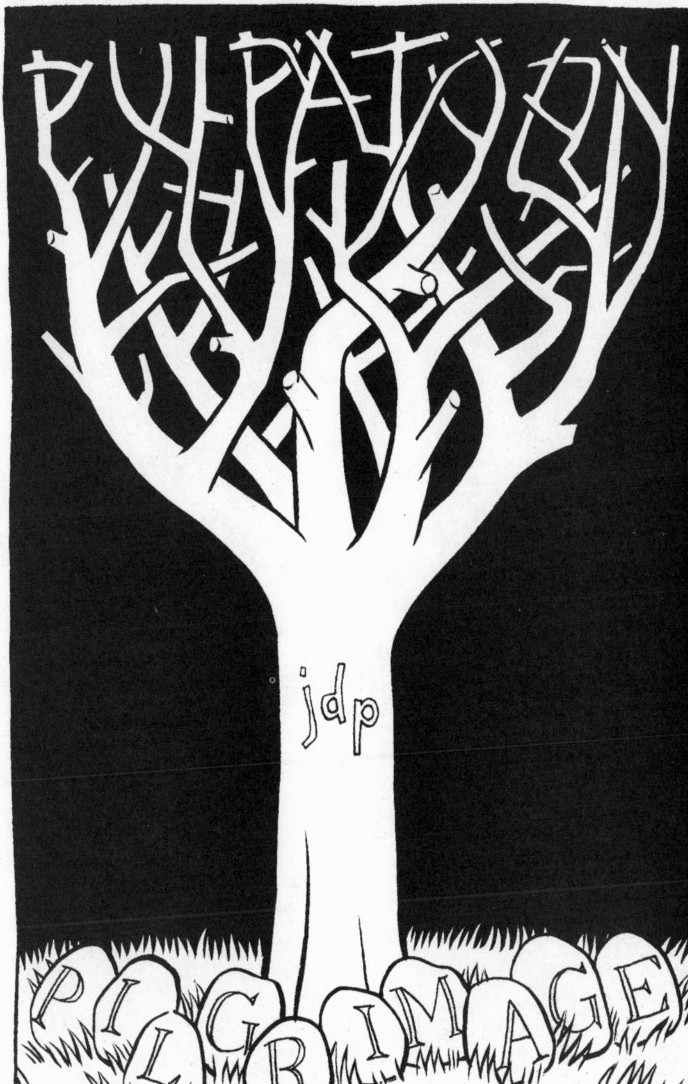

PULPATOON
jdp
PILGRIMAGE

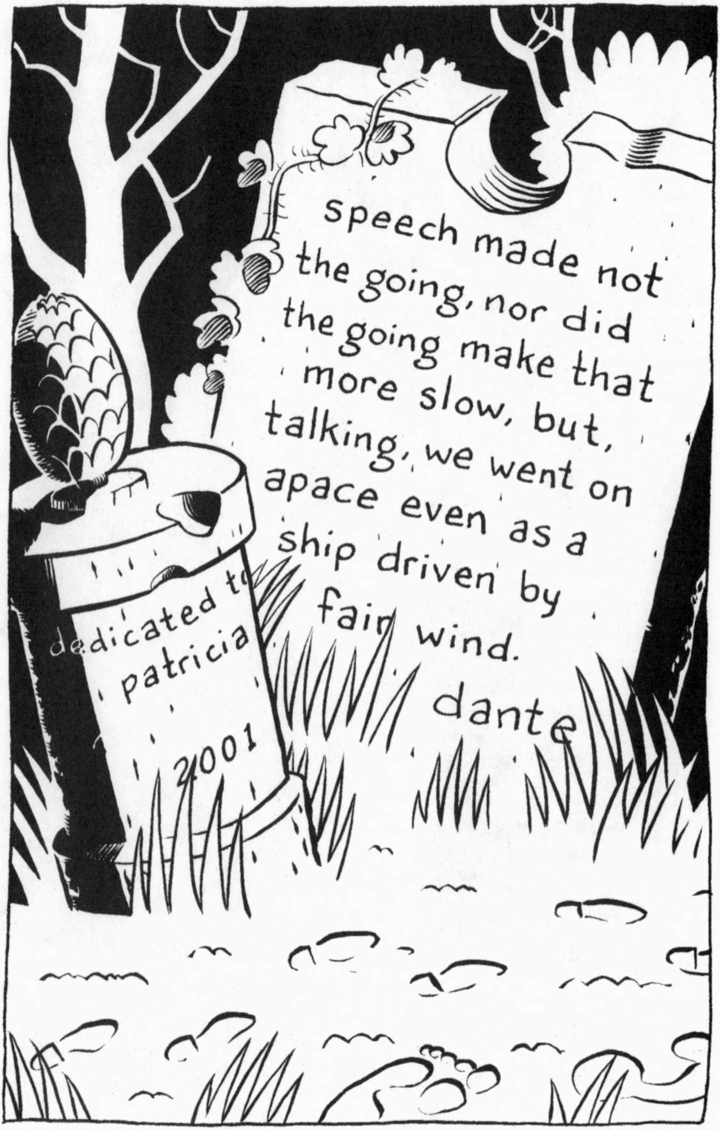
speech made not the going, nor did the going make that more slow, but, talking, we went on apace even as a ship driven by fair wind.
dante
dedicated to patricia
2001

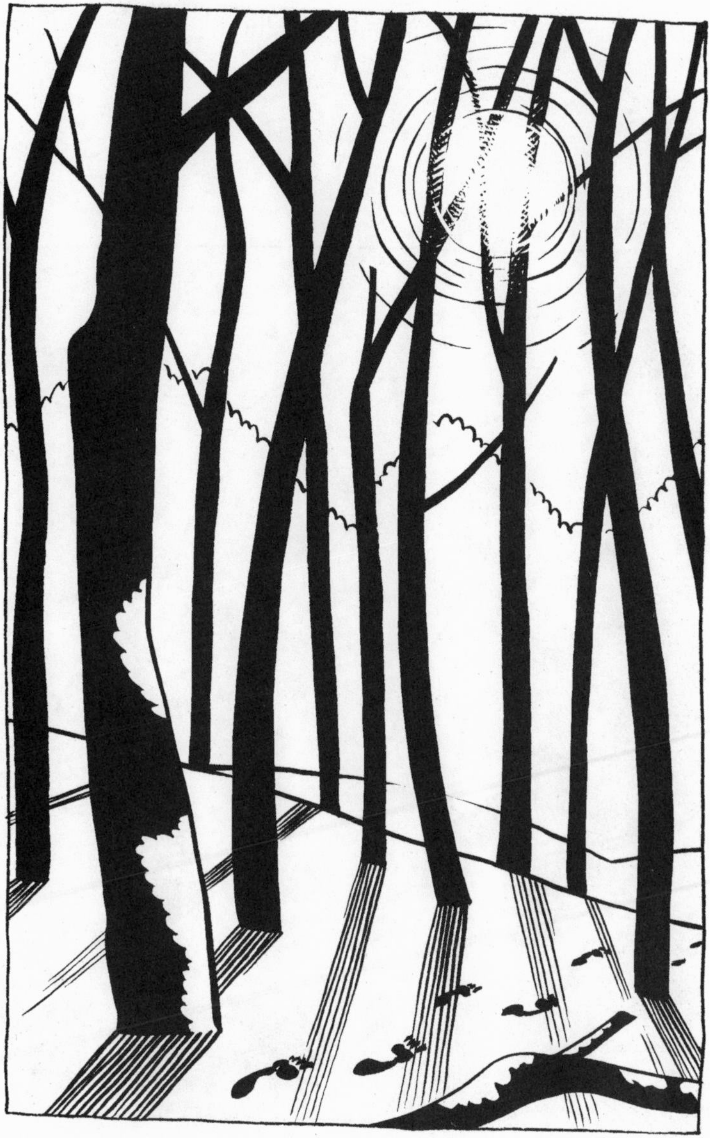

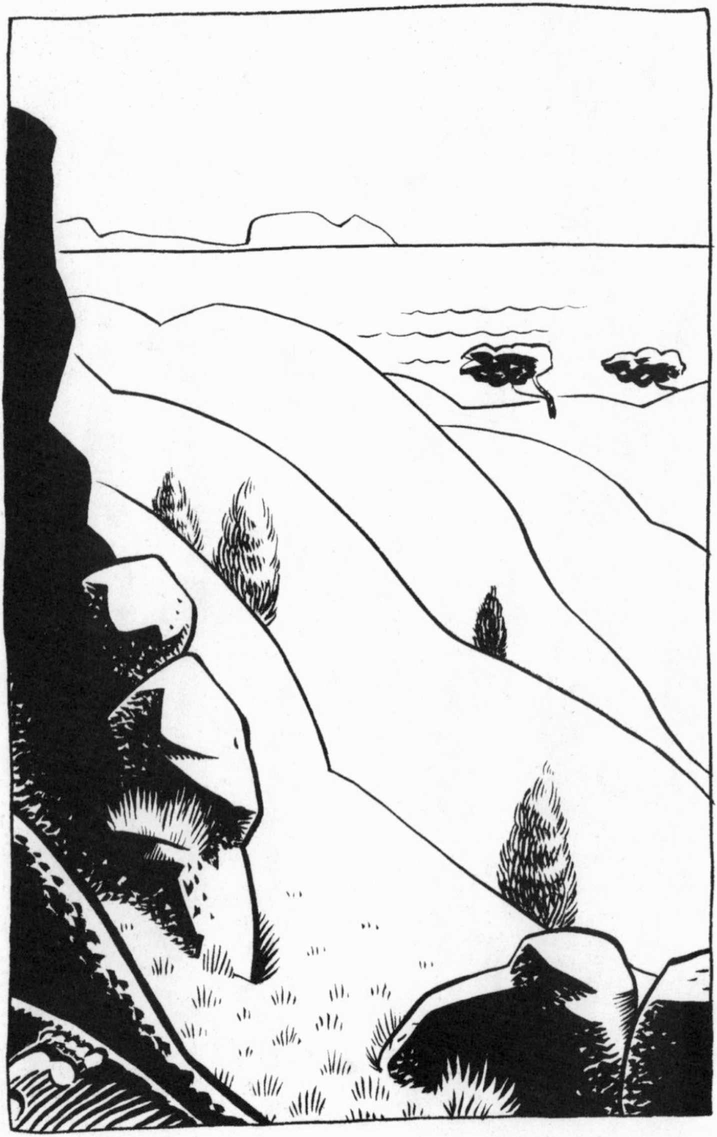

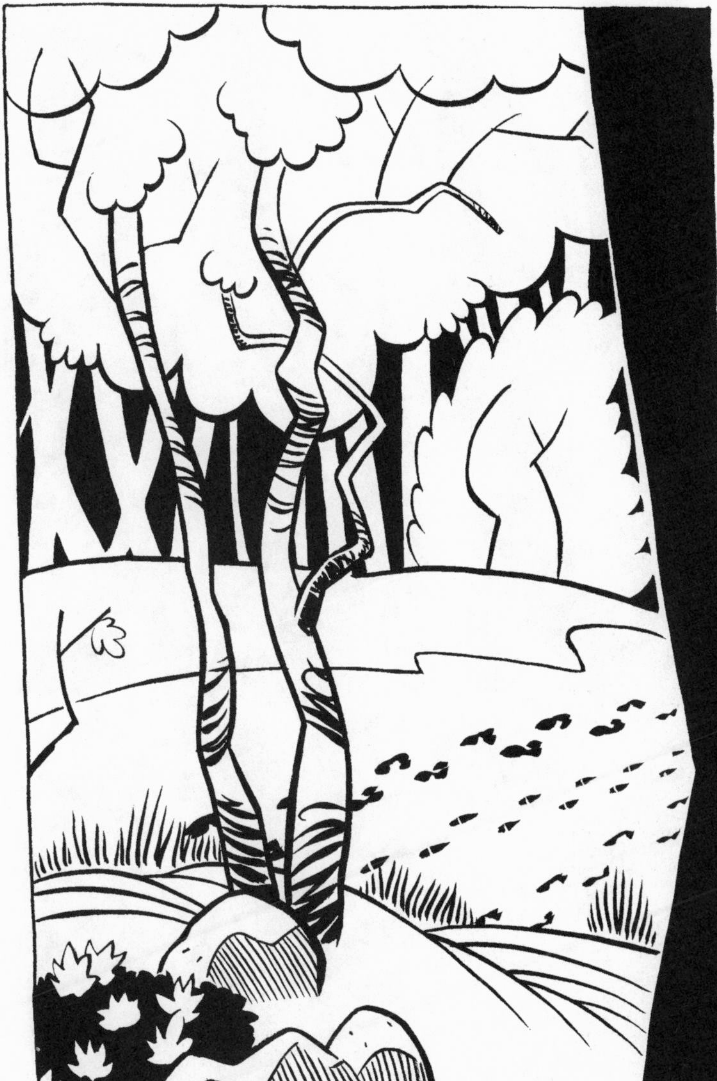

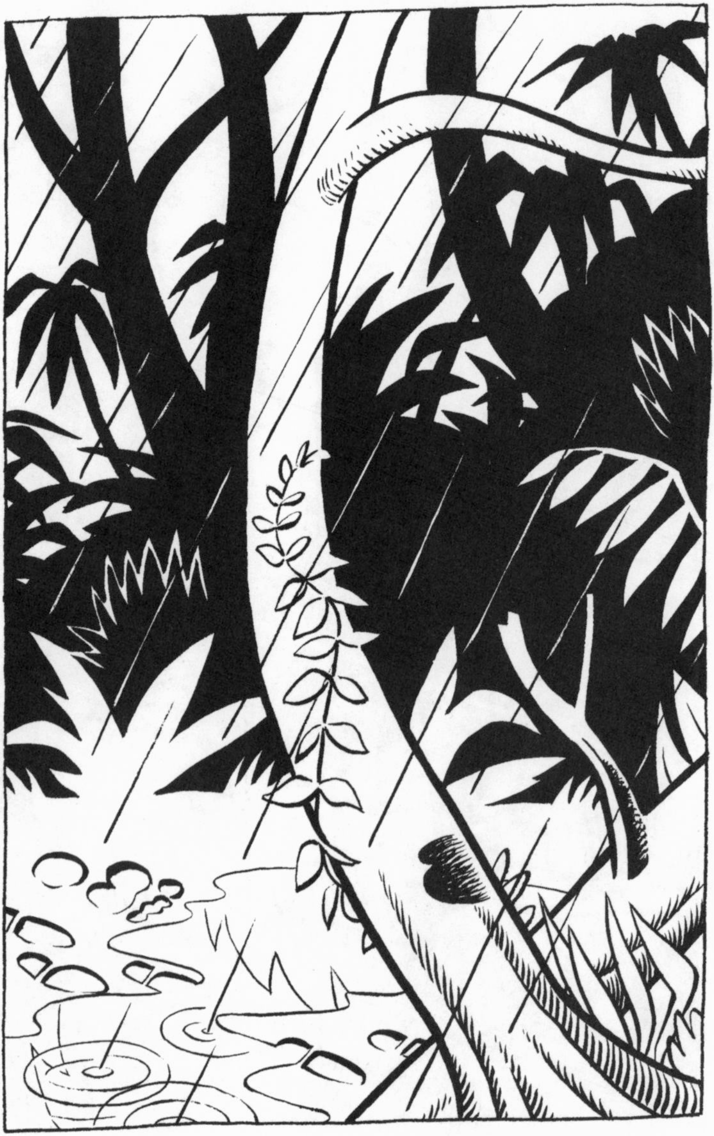

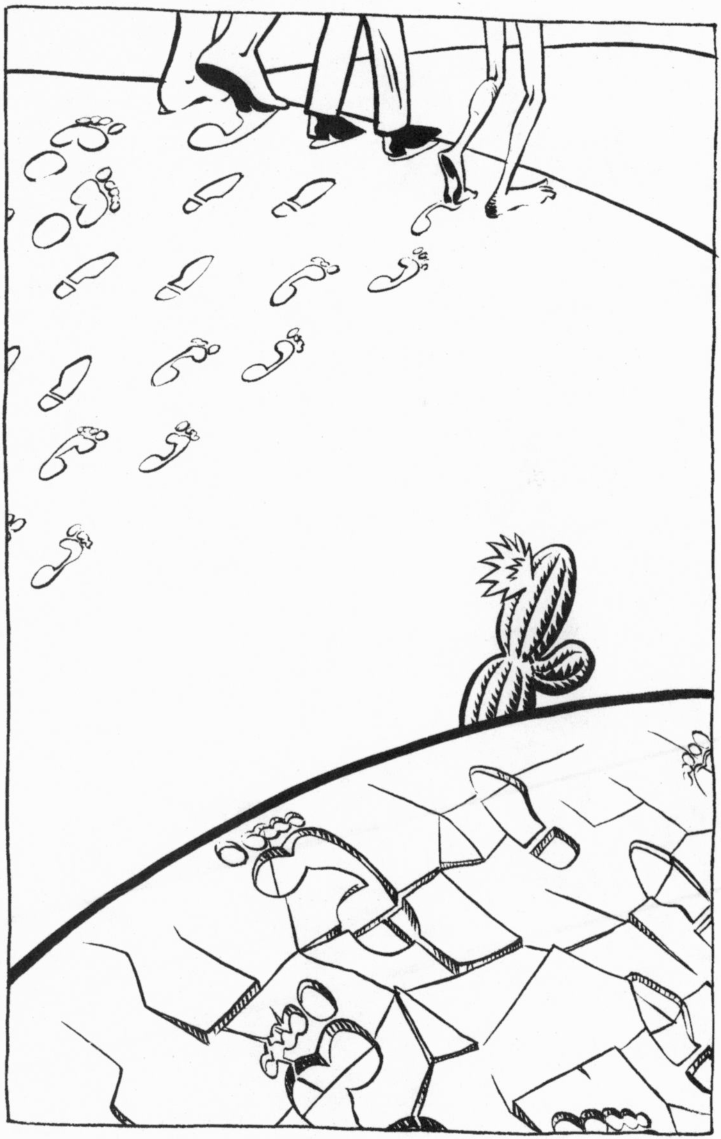

row bot , bull , & delaware thistle

in

honey

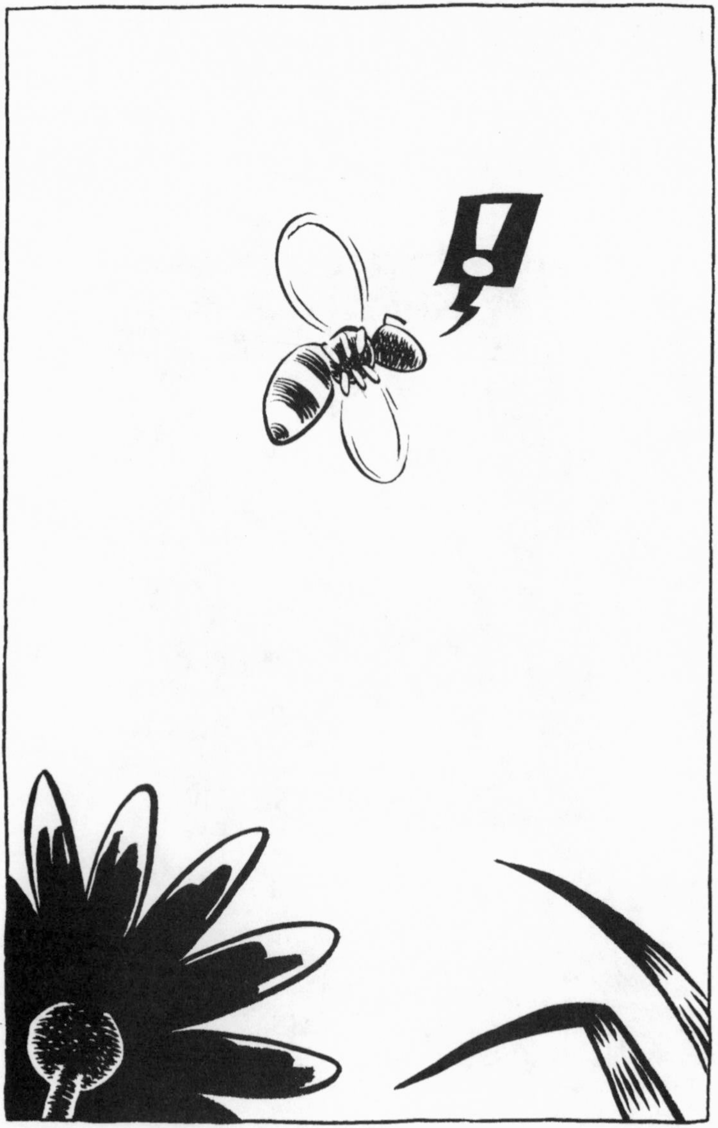

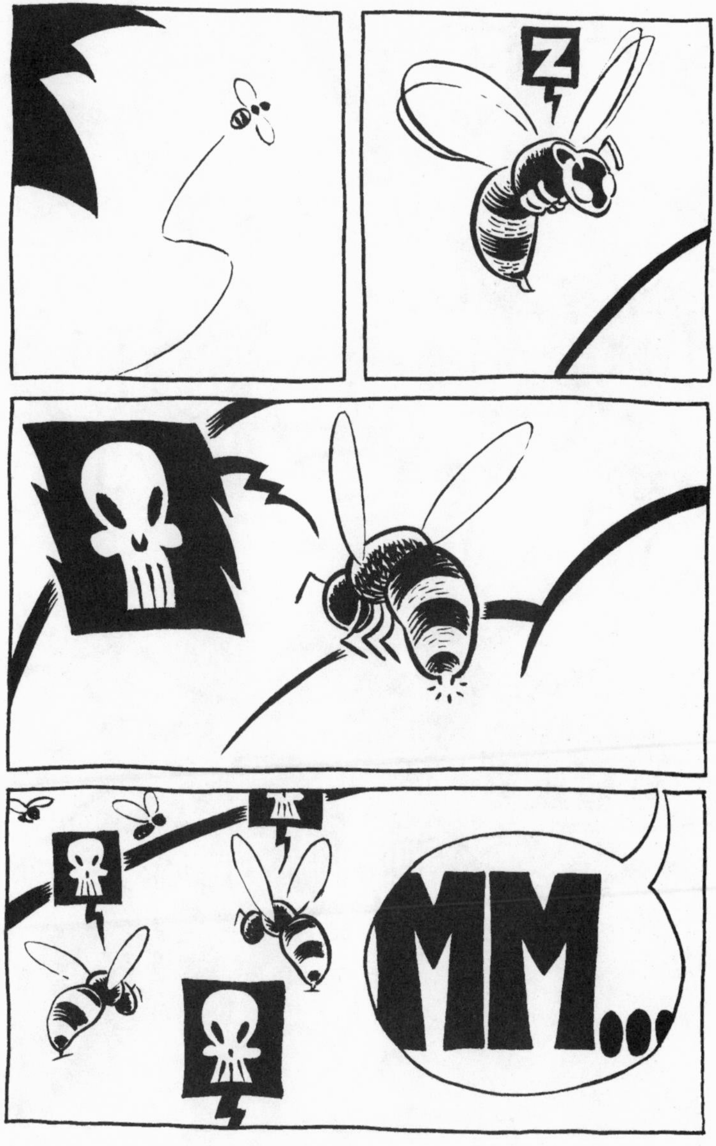
Z
MM...

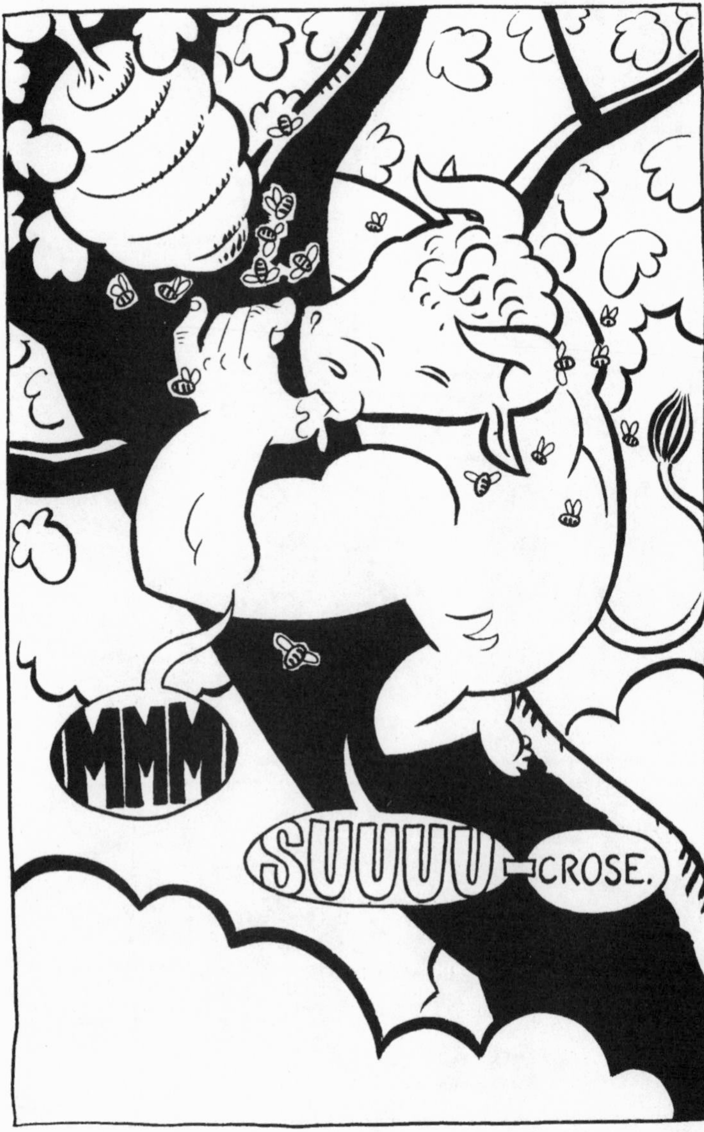
MMM
SUUUU-CROSE.

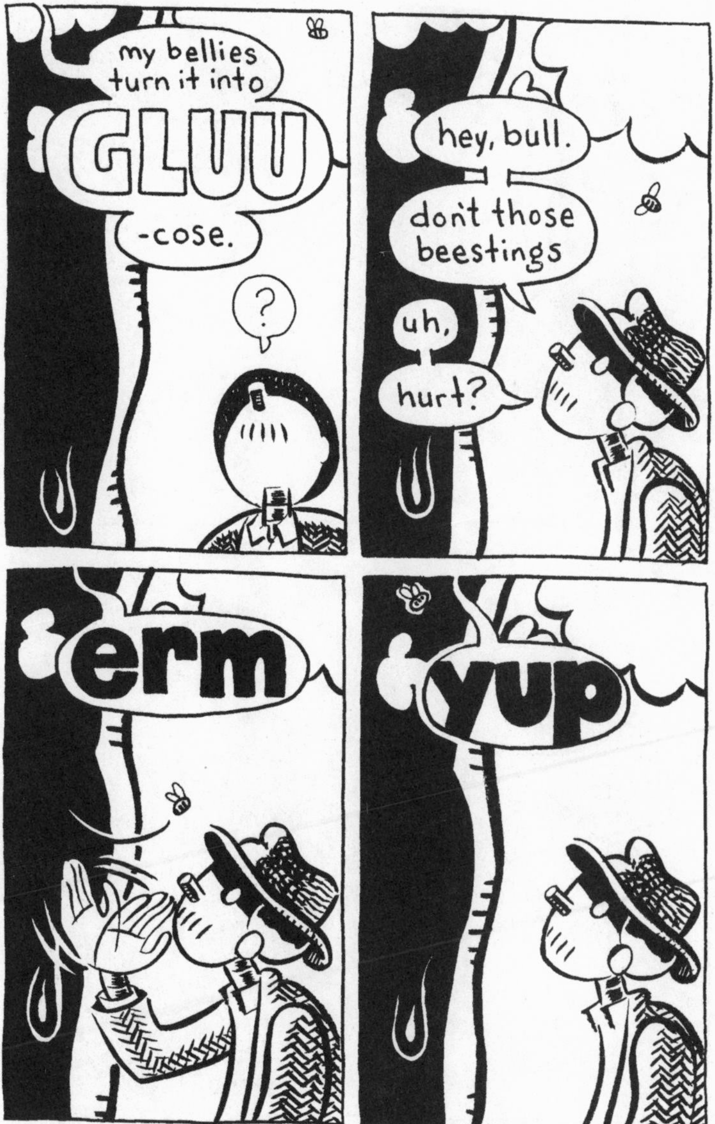
my bellies turn it into
GLUU
-cose.
?
hey, bull.
don't those beestings
uh,
hurt?
erm
yup

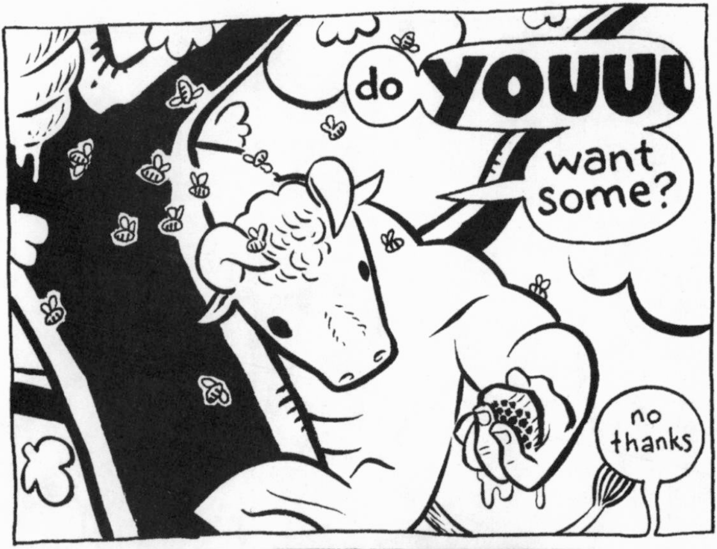
do YOUUU
want some?
no thanks

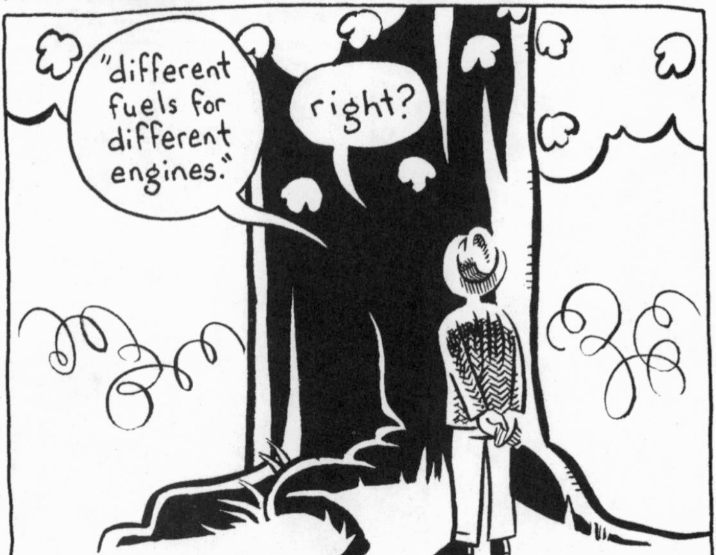
"different fuels for different engines."
right?

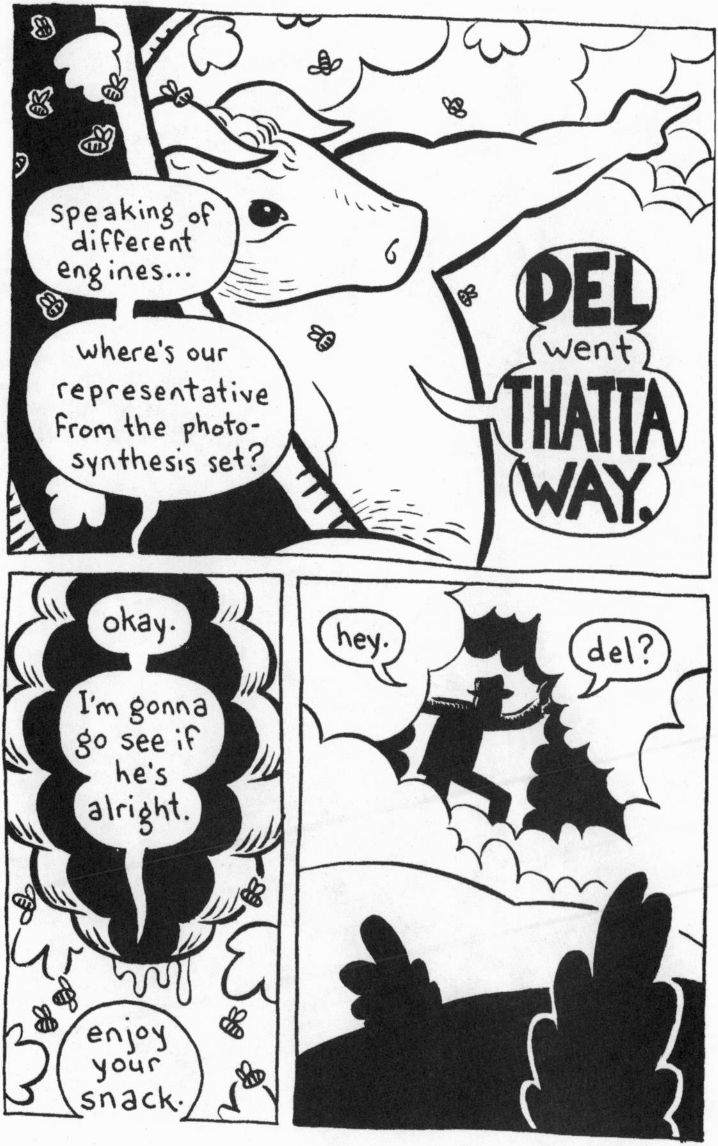

speaking of different engines...
where's our representative from the photo-synthesis set?
DEL went THATTA WAY.
okay.
I'm gonna go see if he's alright.
enjoy your snack.
hey.
del?

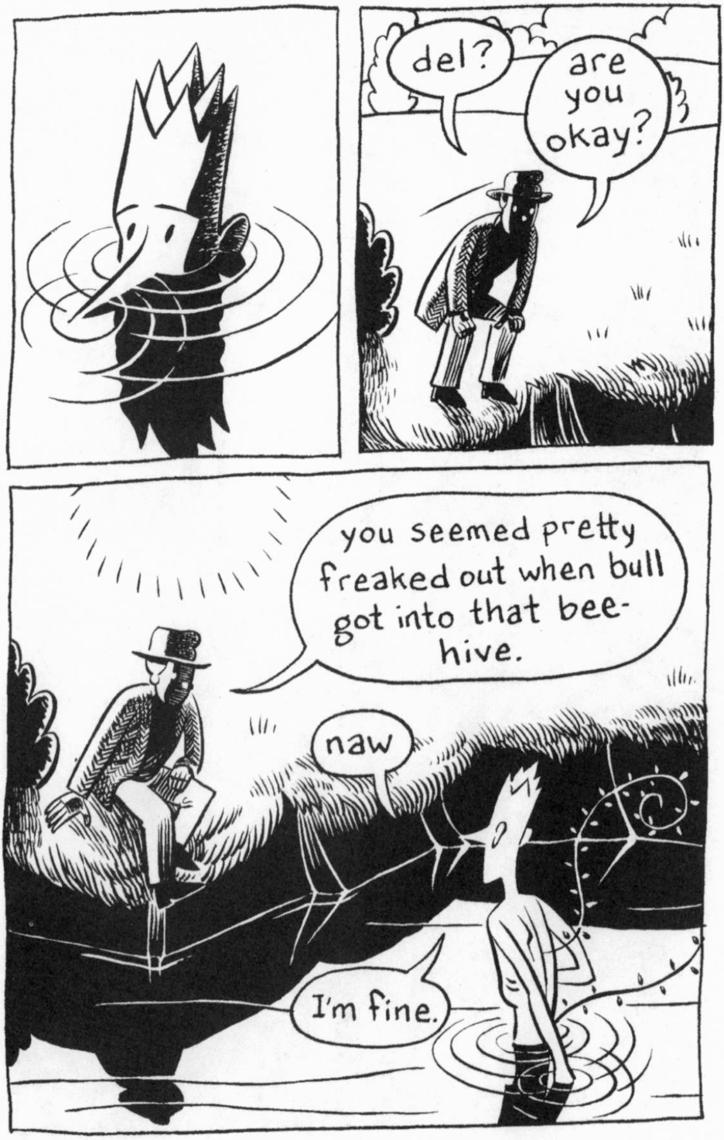
del?
are you okay?
you seemed pretty freaked out when bull got into that bee-hive.
naw
I'm fine.

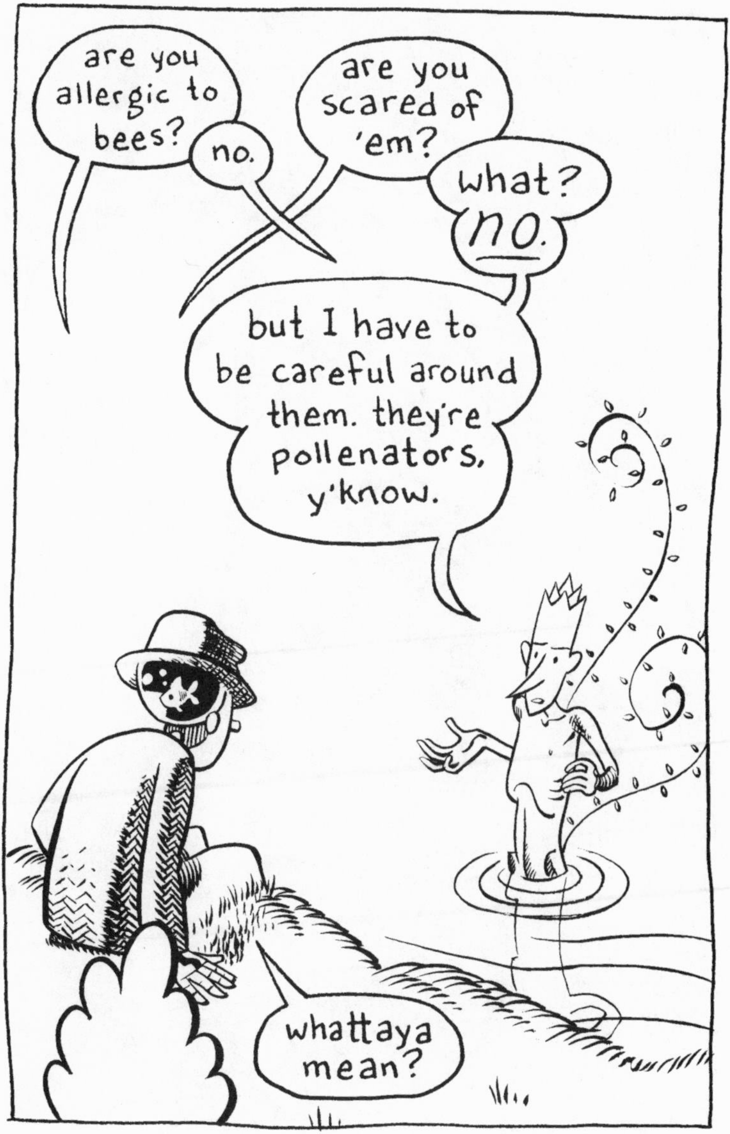
are you allergic to bees?
no.
are you scared of 'em?
what? no.
but I have to be careful around them. they're pollenators, y'know.
whattaya mean?

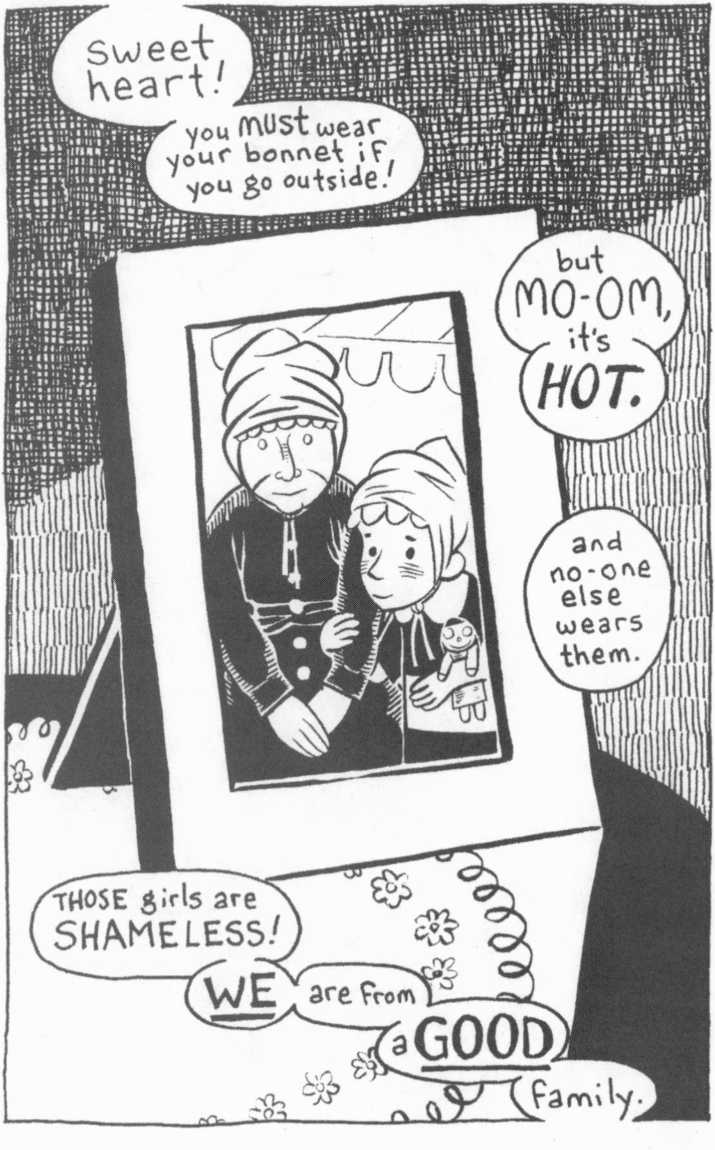
sweet heart!
you MUST wear your bonnet if you go outside!
but MO-OM, it's HOT.
and no-one else wears them.
THOSE girls are SHAMELESS!
WE are from a GOOD family.

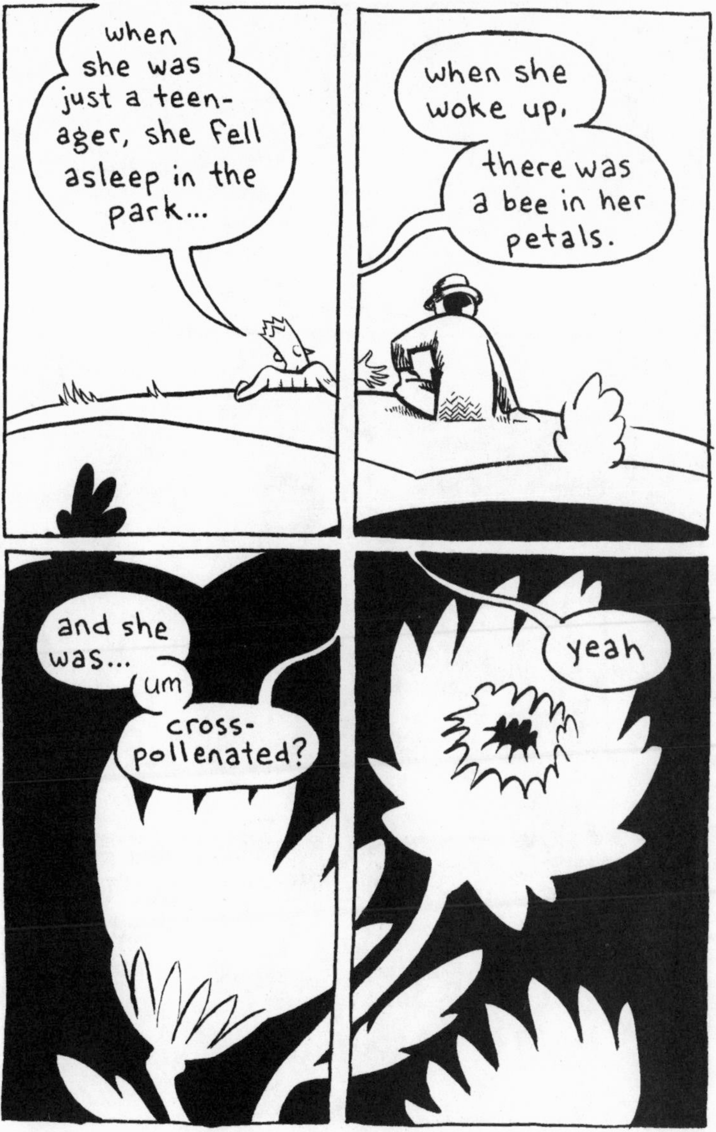
when she was just a teen-ager, she fell asleep in the park...
when she woke up,
there was a bee in her petals.
and she was...
um
cross-pollenated?
yeah

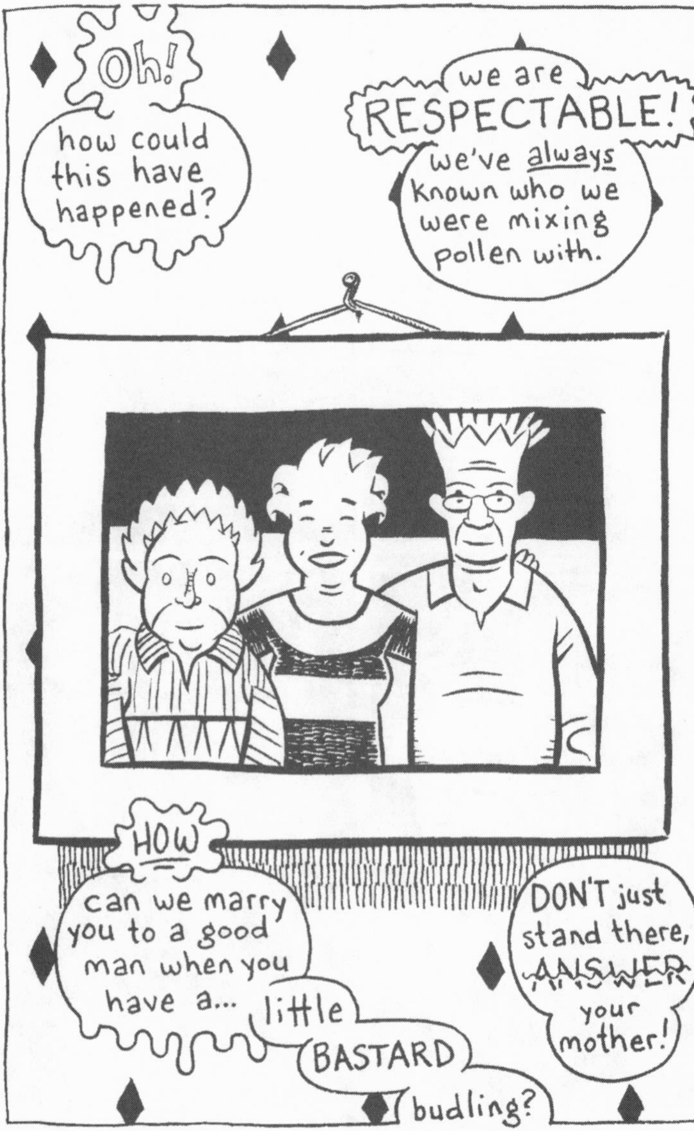
Oh!
how could this have happened?
we are RESPECTABLE!
we've always known who we were mixing pollen with.
HOW can we marry you to a good man when you have a... little BASTARD budling?
DON'T just stand there, ANSWER your mother!

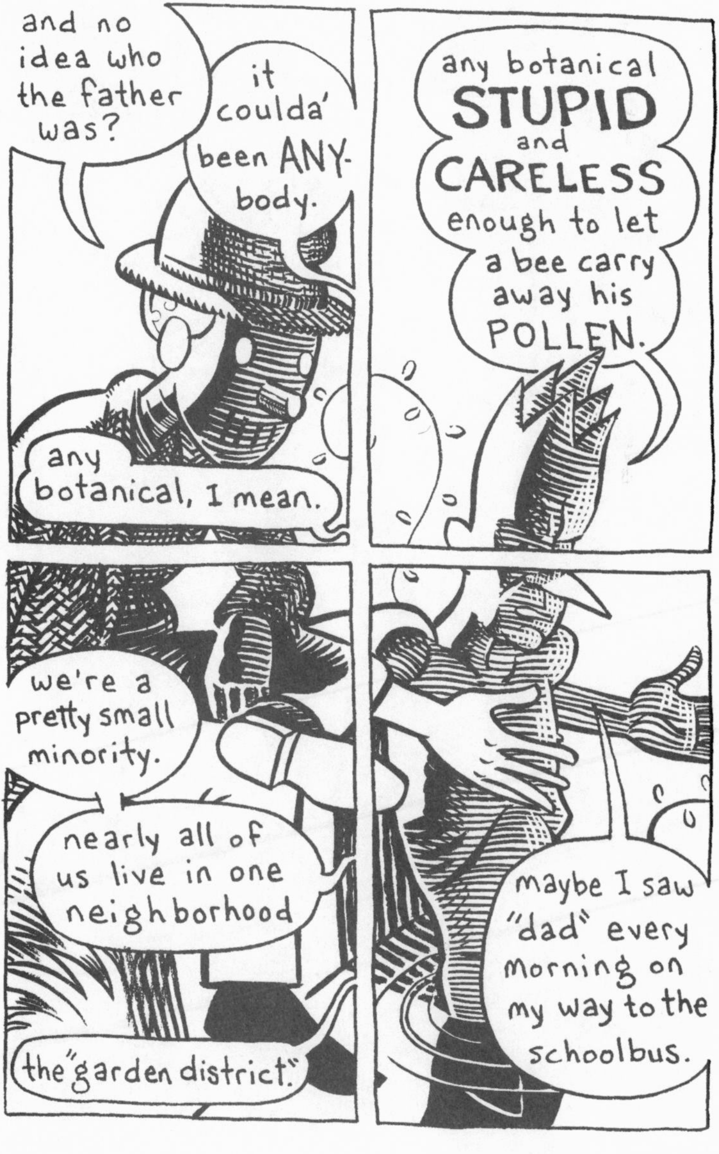
and no idea who the father was?
it coulda' been ANY-body.
any botanical, I mean.
any botanical STUPID and CARELESS enough to let a bee carry away his POLLEN.
we're a pretty small minority.
nearly all of us live in one neighborhood
the "garden district".
maybe I saw "dad" every morning on my way to the schoolbus.

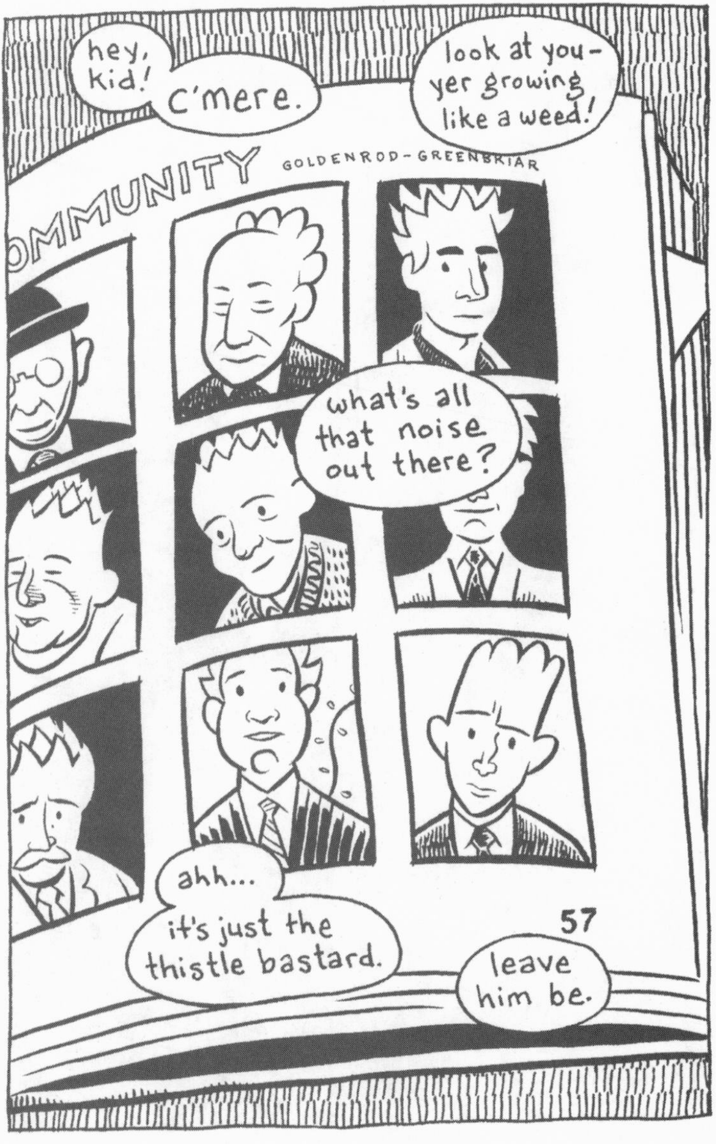
hey, kid!
c'mere.
look at you- yer growing like a weed!
COMMUNITY
GOLDENROD-GREENBRIAR
what's all that noise out there?
ahh...
it's just the thistle bastard.
57
leave him be.

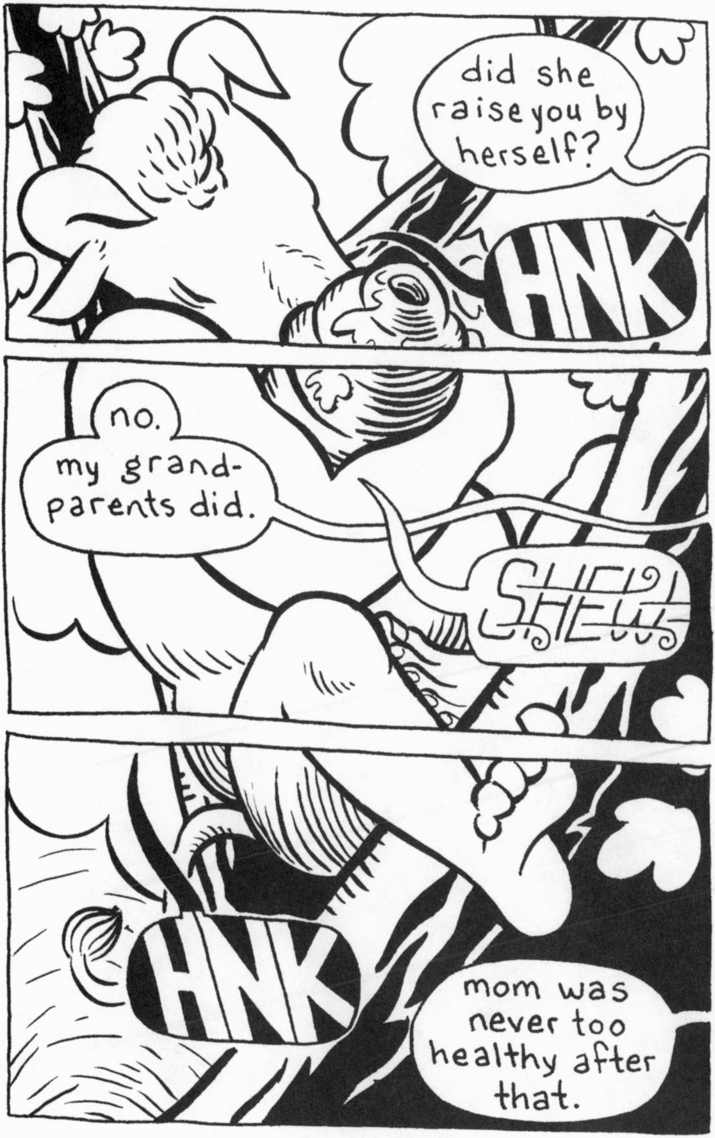
did she raise you by herself?
HNK
no. my grand-parents did.
SHEW
HNK
mom was never too healthy after that.

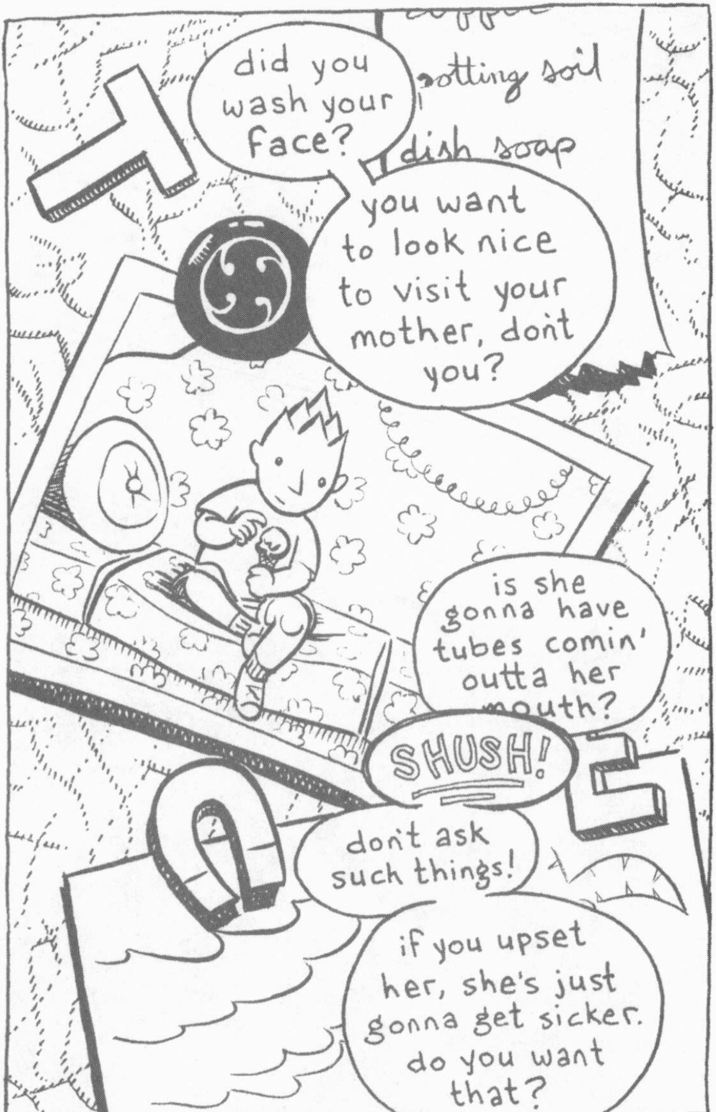
did you wash your face?
otting soil
dish soap
you want to look nice to visit your mother, don't you?
is she gonna have tubes comin' outta her mouth?
SHUSH!
don't ask such things!
if you upset her, she's just gonna get sicker. do you want that?

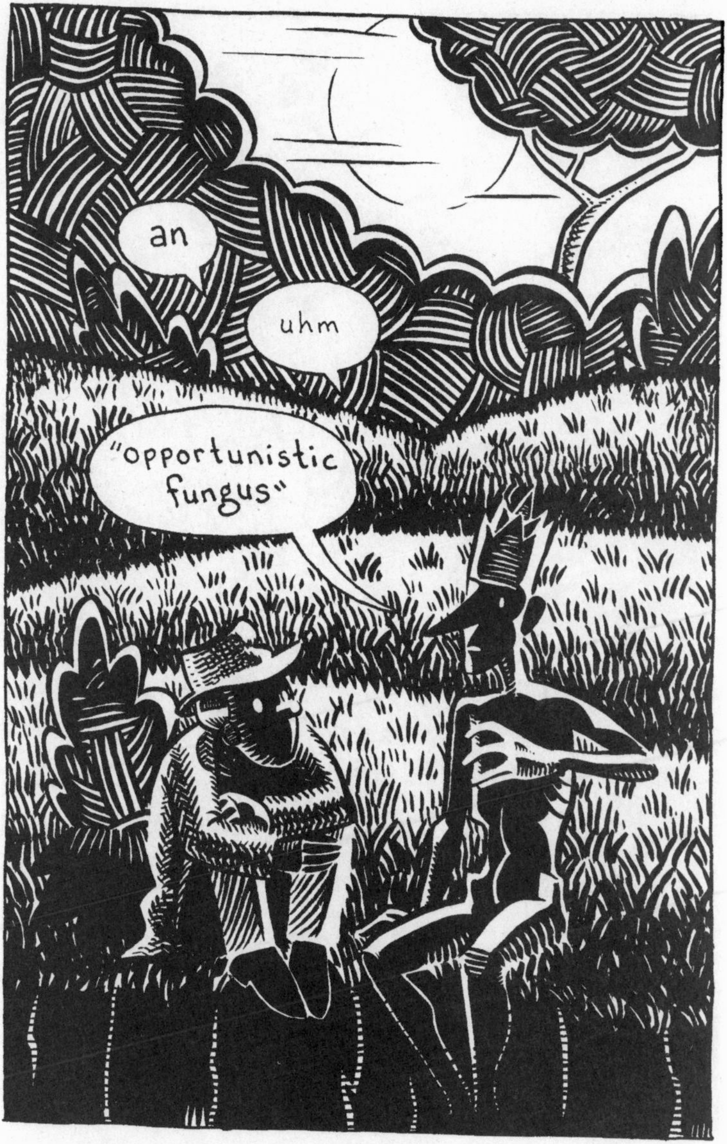
an
uhm
"opportunistic fungus"

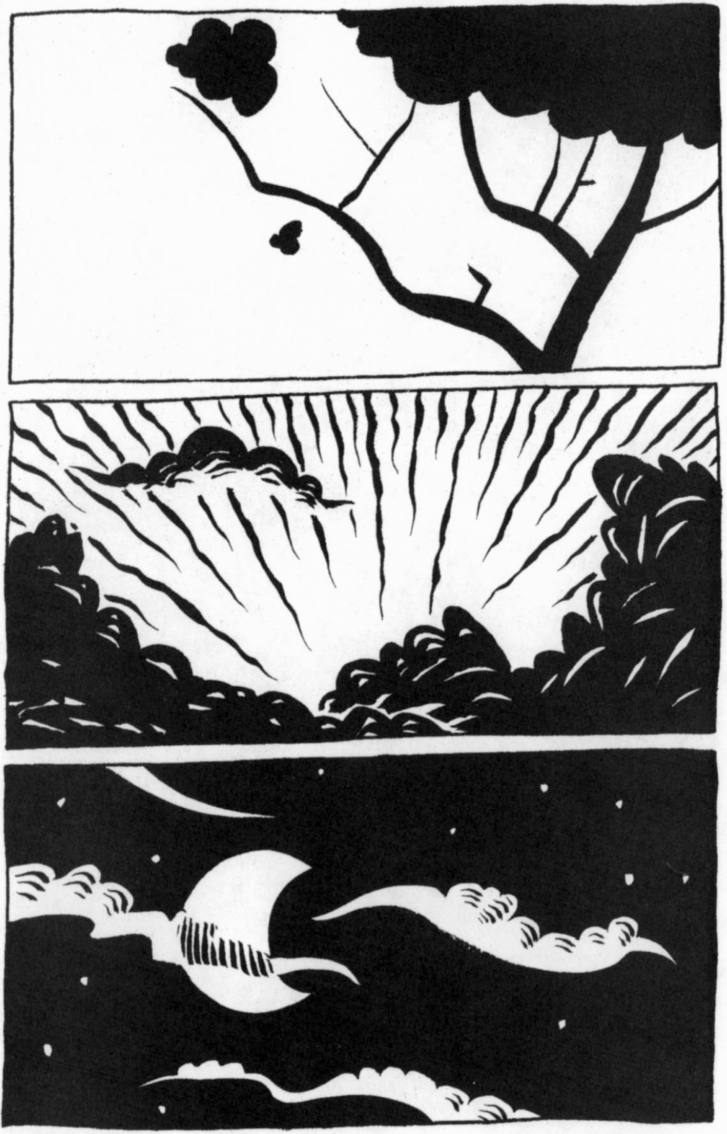

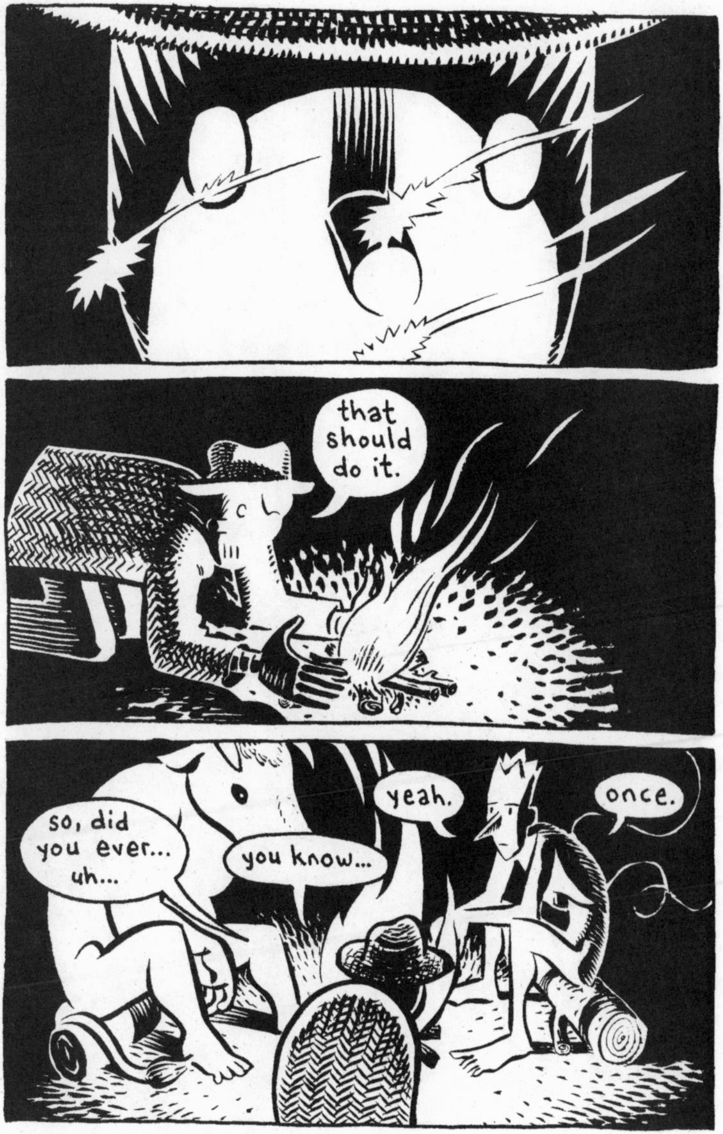
that should do it.
so, did you ever... uh...
you know...
yeah.
once.

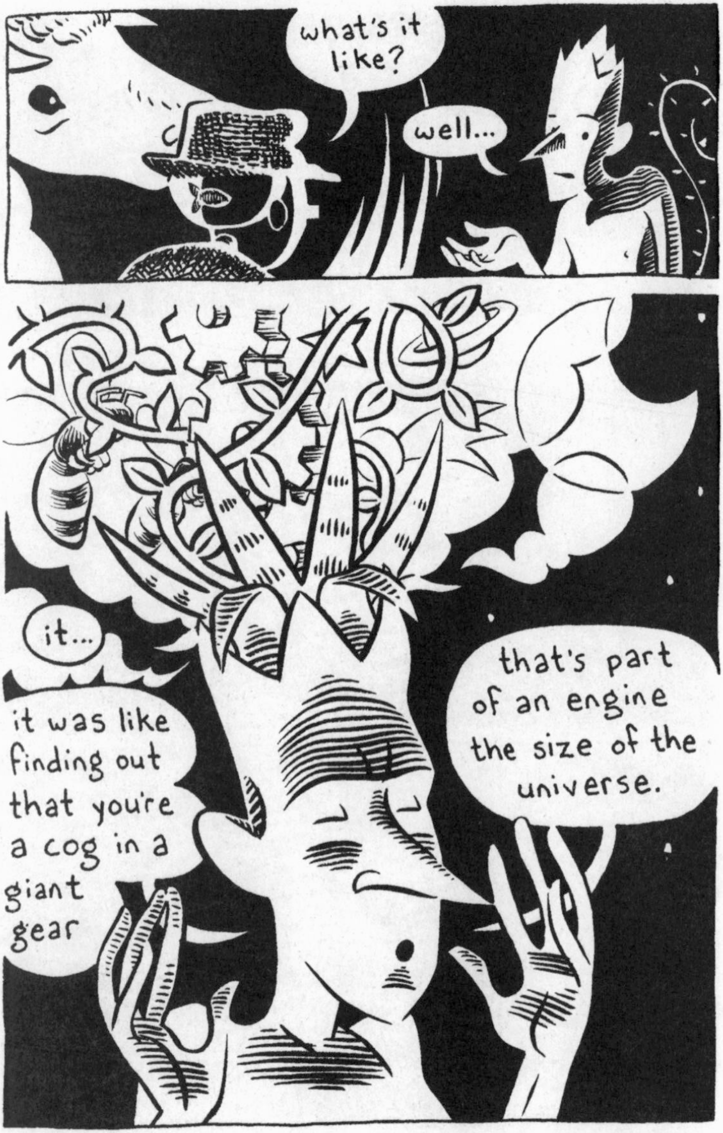
what's it like?
well...
it...
it was like finding out that you're a cog in a giant gear
that's part of an engine the size of the universe.

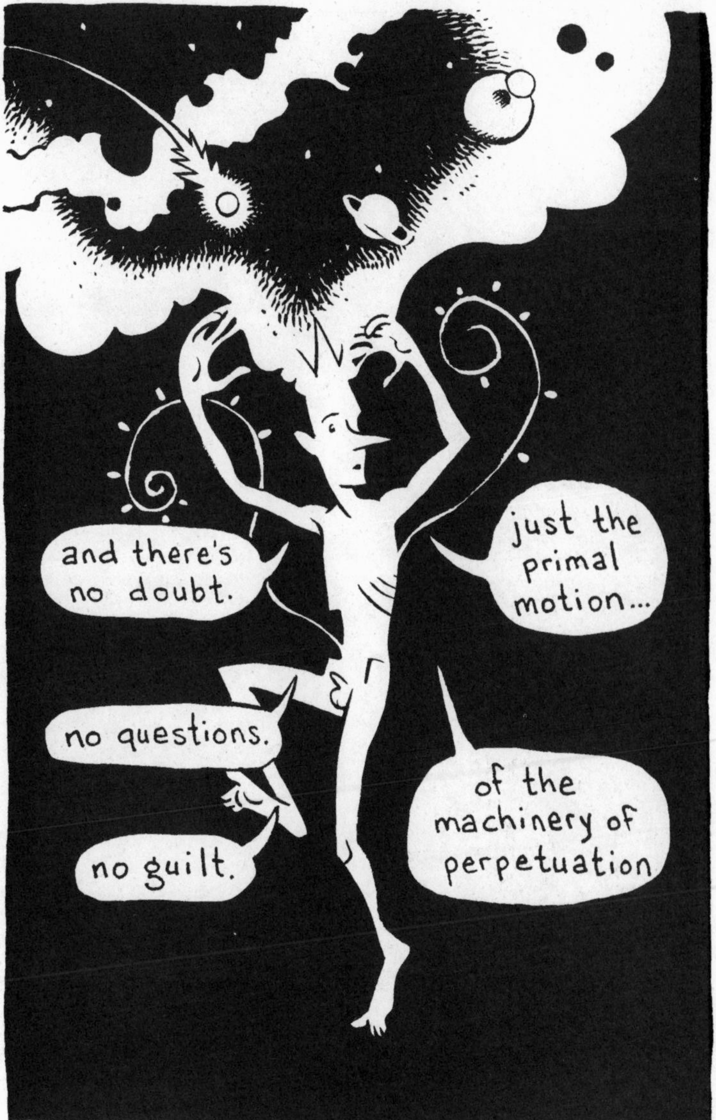

and there's no doubt.
just the primal motion...
no questions.
of the machinery of perpetuation
no guilt.

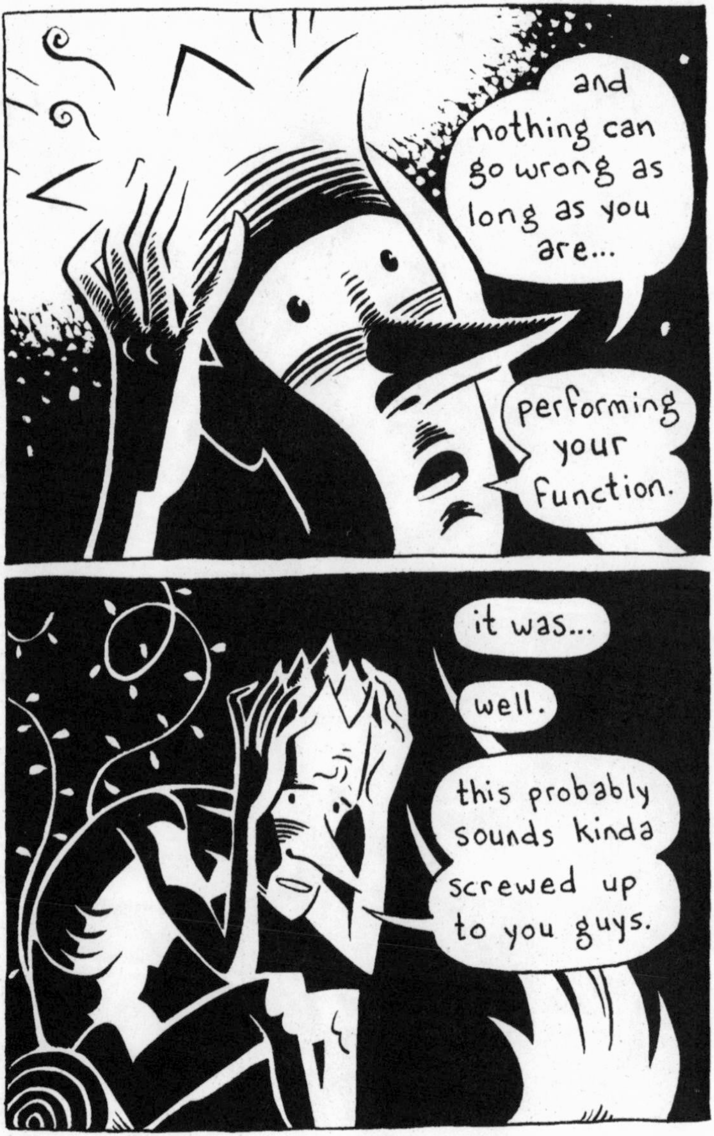
and nothing can go wrong as long as you are...
performing your function.
it was...
well.
this probably sounds kinda screwed up to you guys.

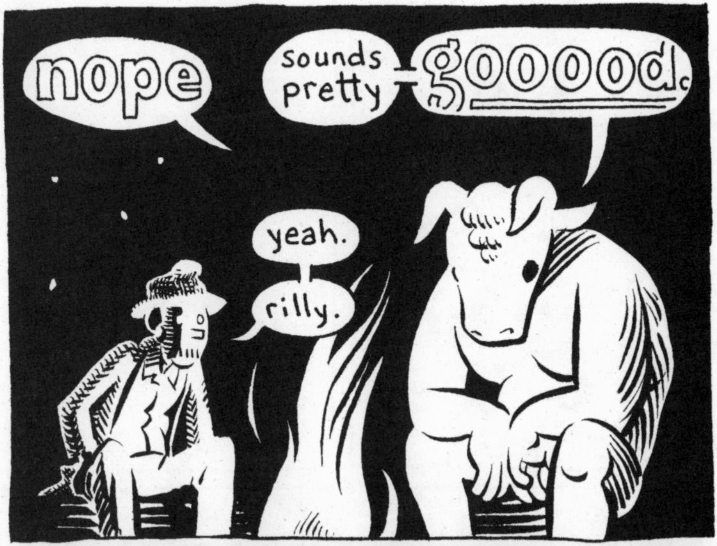
nope
sounds pretty goooood.
yeah.
rilly.

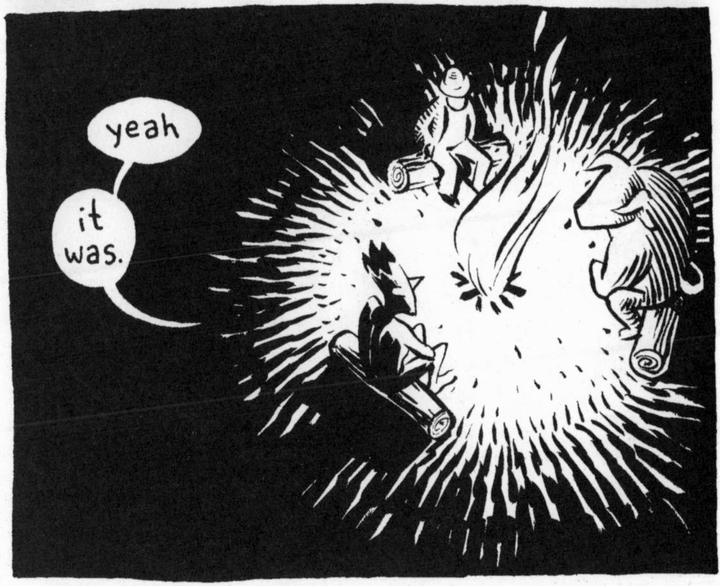
yeah
it was.

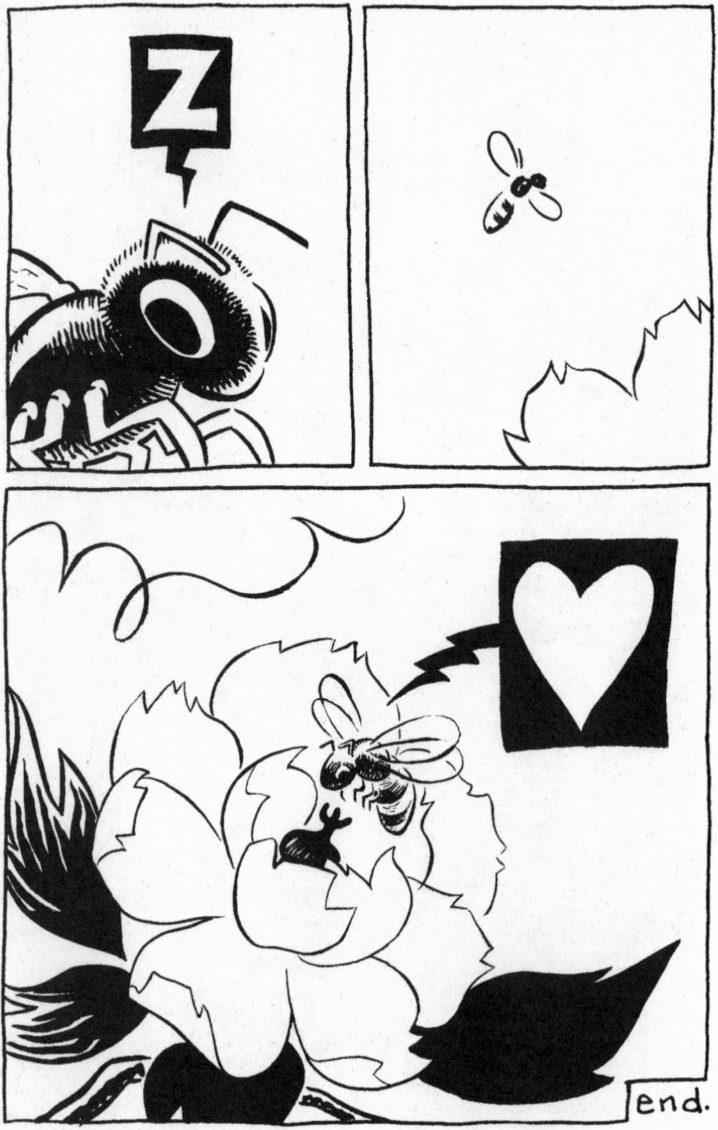
Z
end.

rowbot, bull & delaware thistle

in

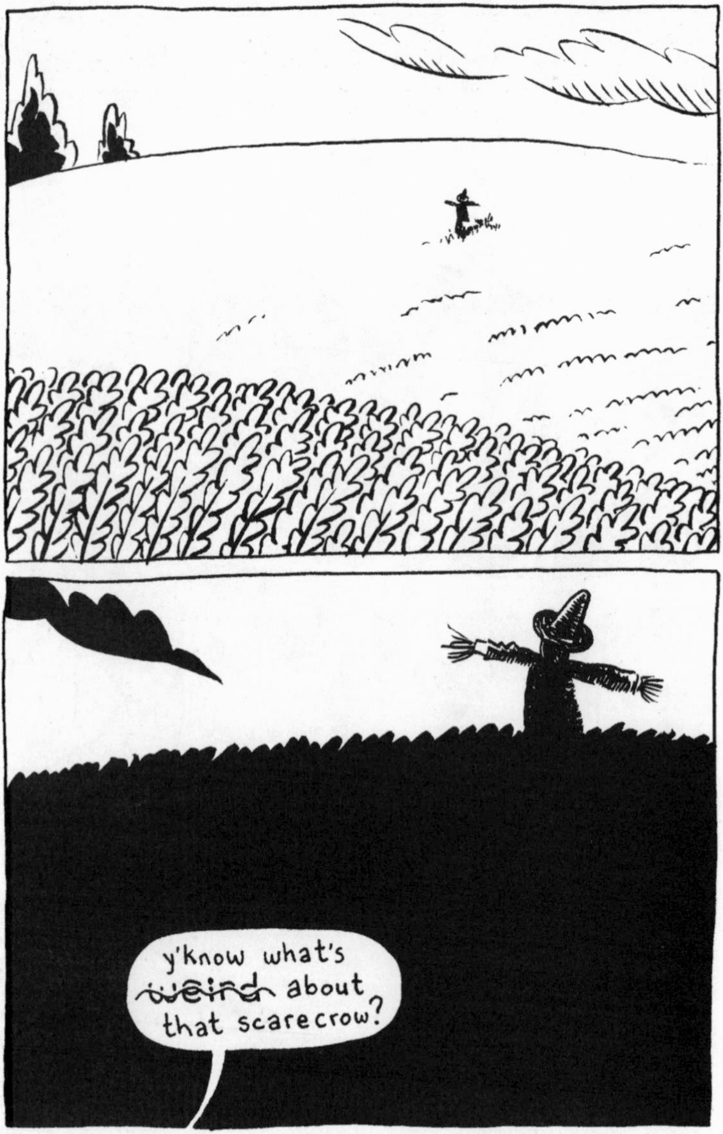
y'know what's weird about that scarecrow?

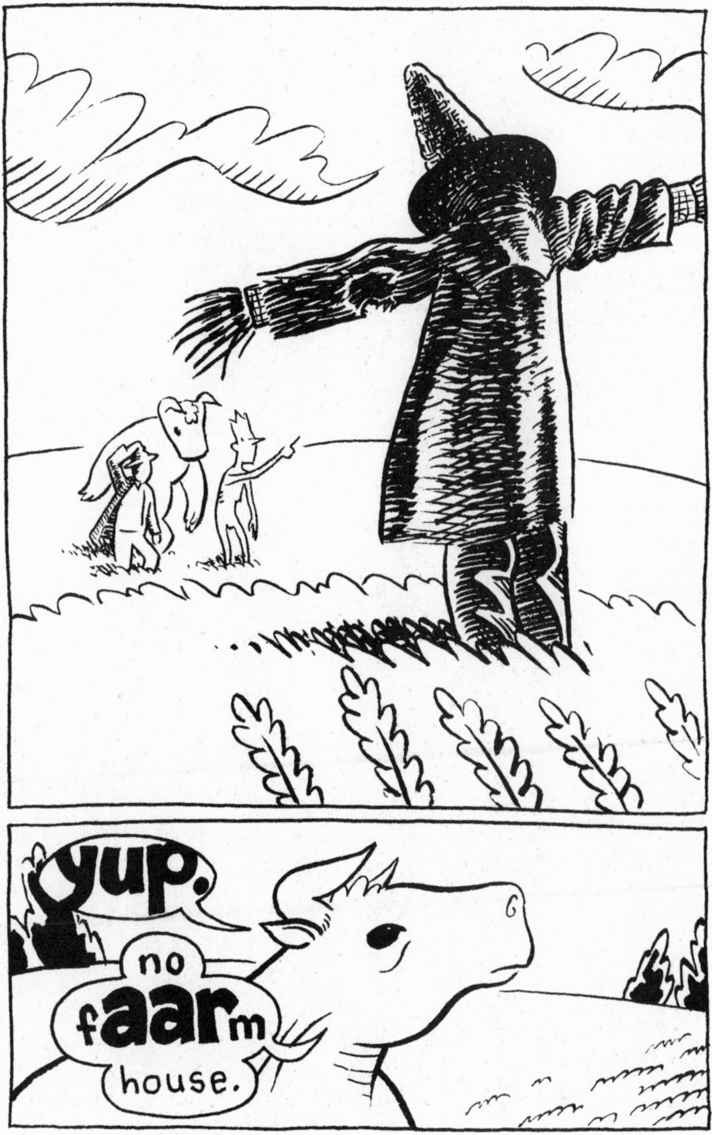
yup.
no faarm house.

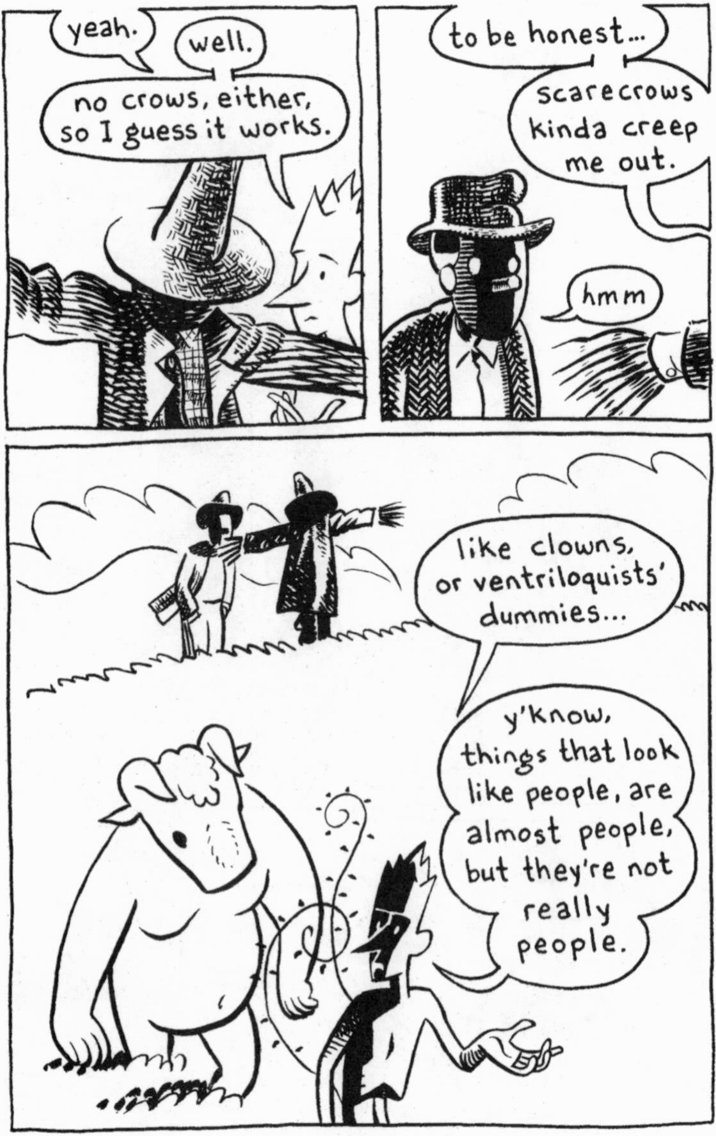
yeah.
well.
no crows, either, so I guess it works.
to be honest...
scarecrows kinda creep me out.
hmm
like clowns, or ventriloquists' dummies...
y'know, things that look like people, are almost people, but they're not really people.

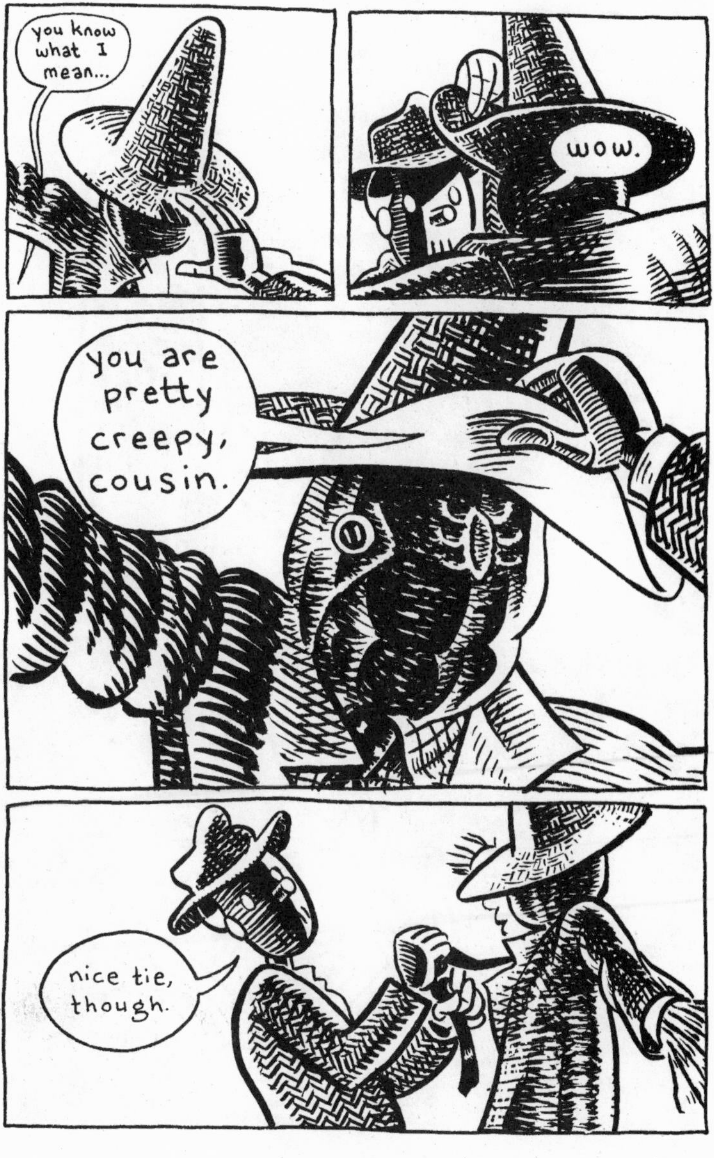
you know what I mean...
wow.
you are pretty creepy, cousin.
nice tie, though.

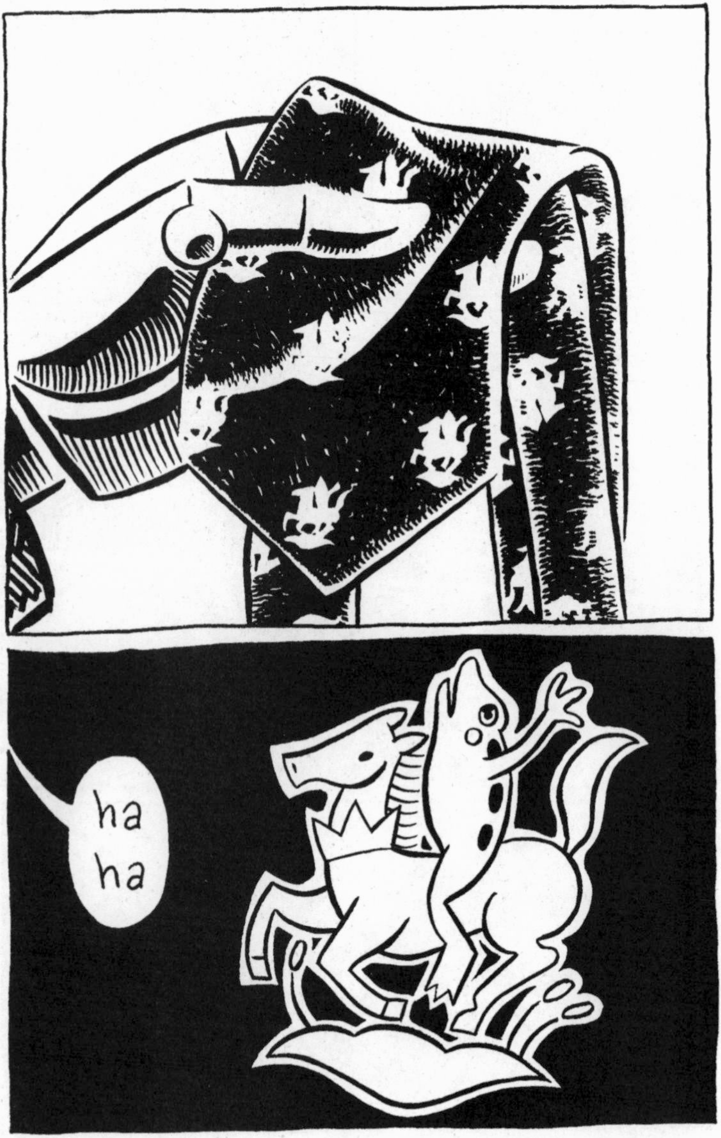
ha ha

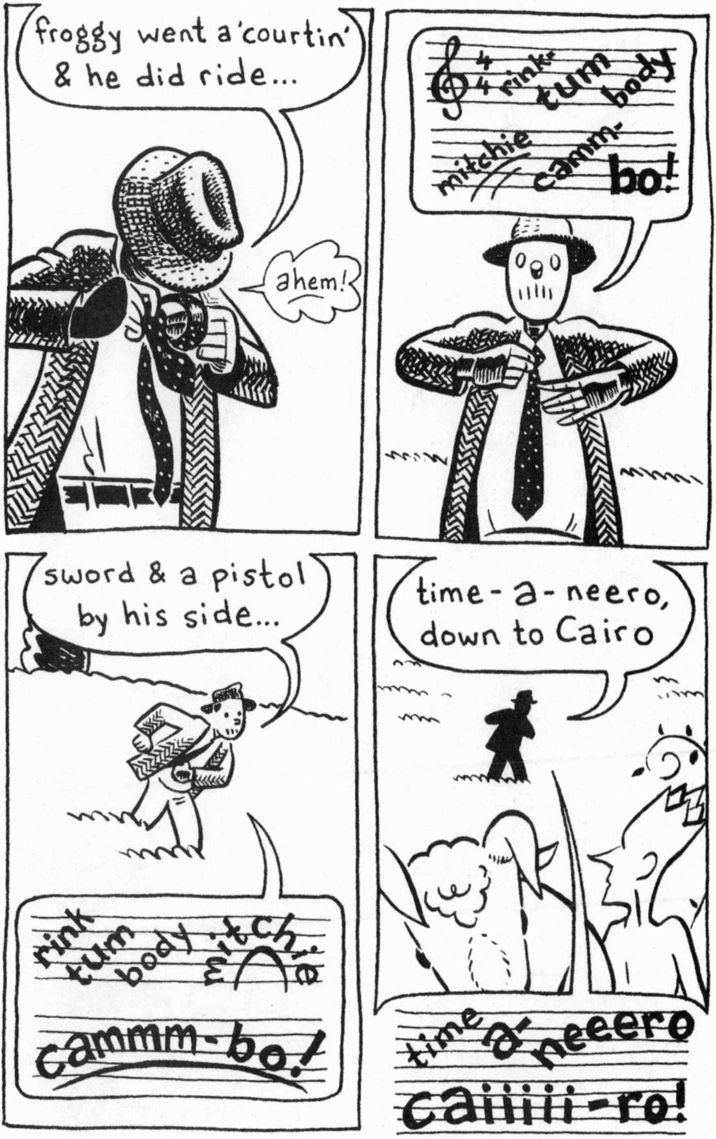
froggy went a 'courtin' & he did ride...
ahem!
rink tum body mitchie camm-bo!
sword & a pistol by his side...
rink tum body mitchie cammmm-bo!
time-a-neero, down to Cairo
time a' neeero caiiiii-ro!

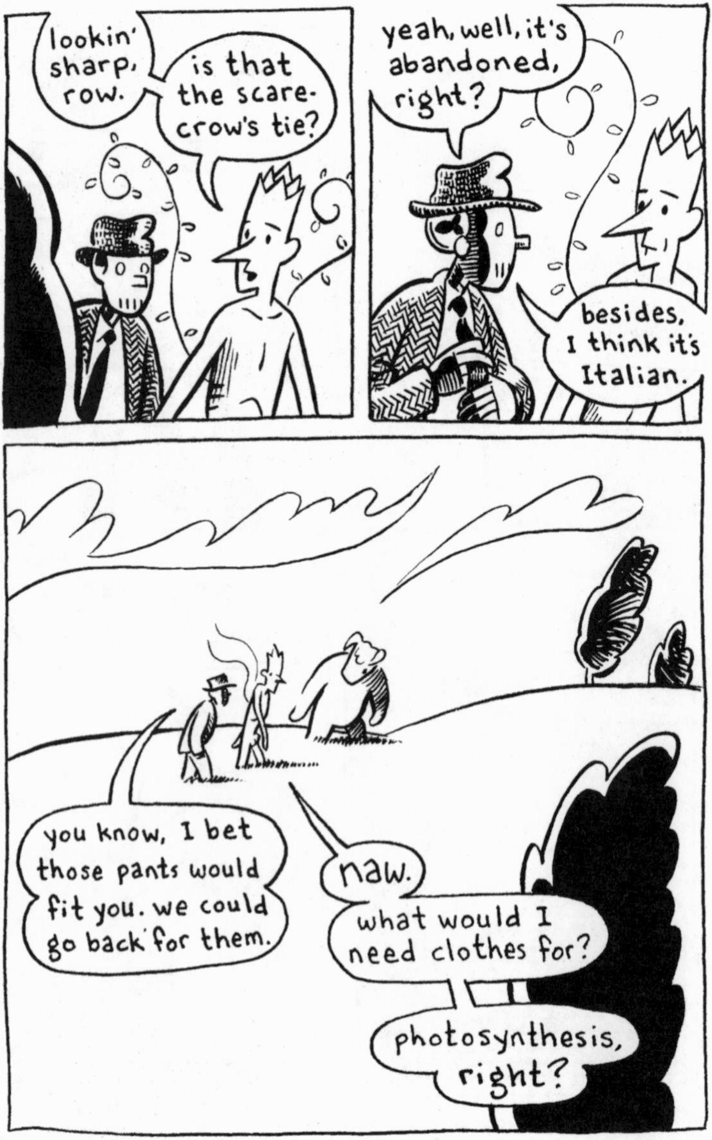
lookin' sharp, row.
is that the scare-crow's tie?
yeah, well, it's abandoned, right?
besides, I think it's Italian.
you know, I bet those pants would fit you. we could go back for them.
naw.
what would I need clothes for?
photosynthesis, right?

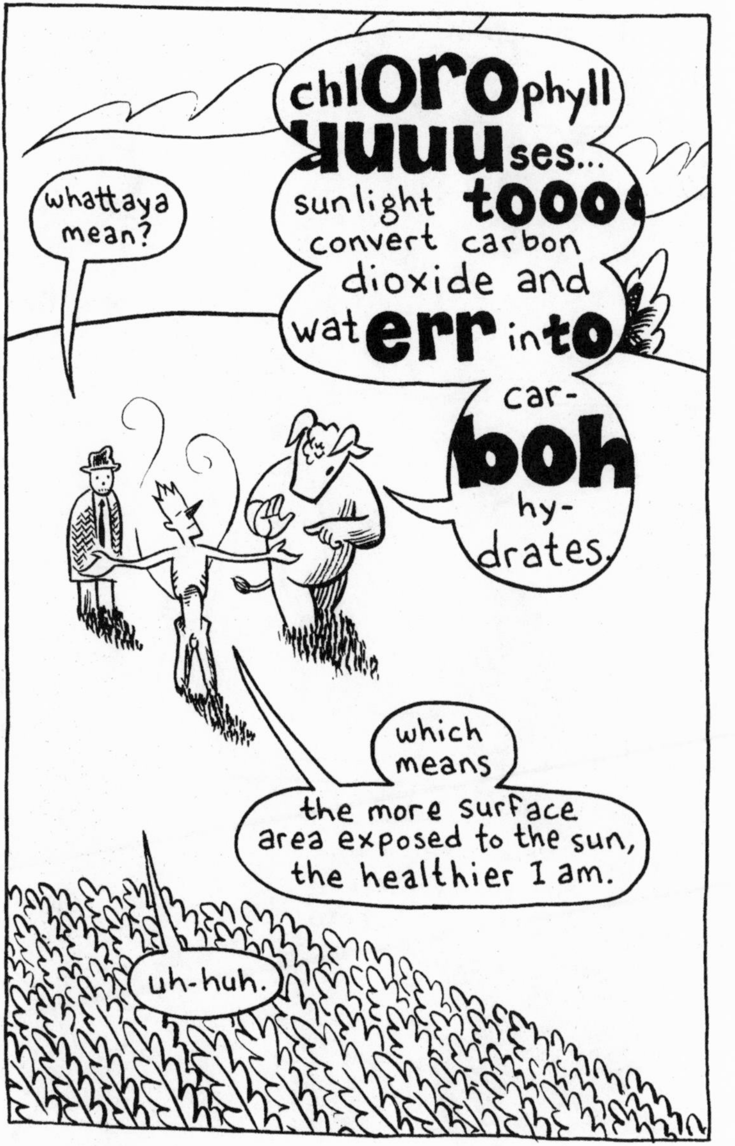
chlOROphyll UUUUses... sunlight toooo convert carbon dioxide and watERR inTO car-BOH hy-drates.
whattaya mean?
which means the more surface area exposed to the sun, the healthier I am.
uh-huh.

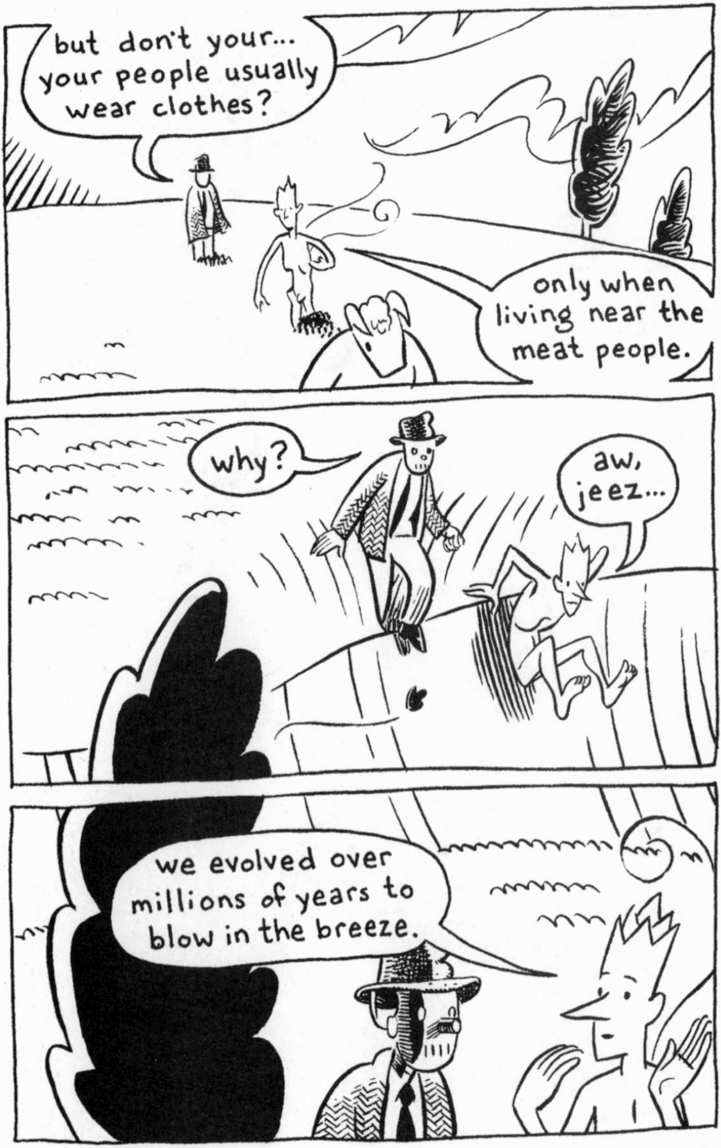
but don't your... your people usually wear clothes?
only when living near the meat people.
why?
aw, jeez...
we evolved over millions of years to blow in the breeze.

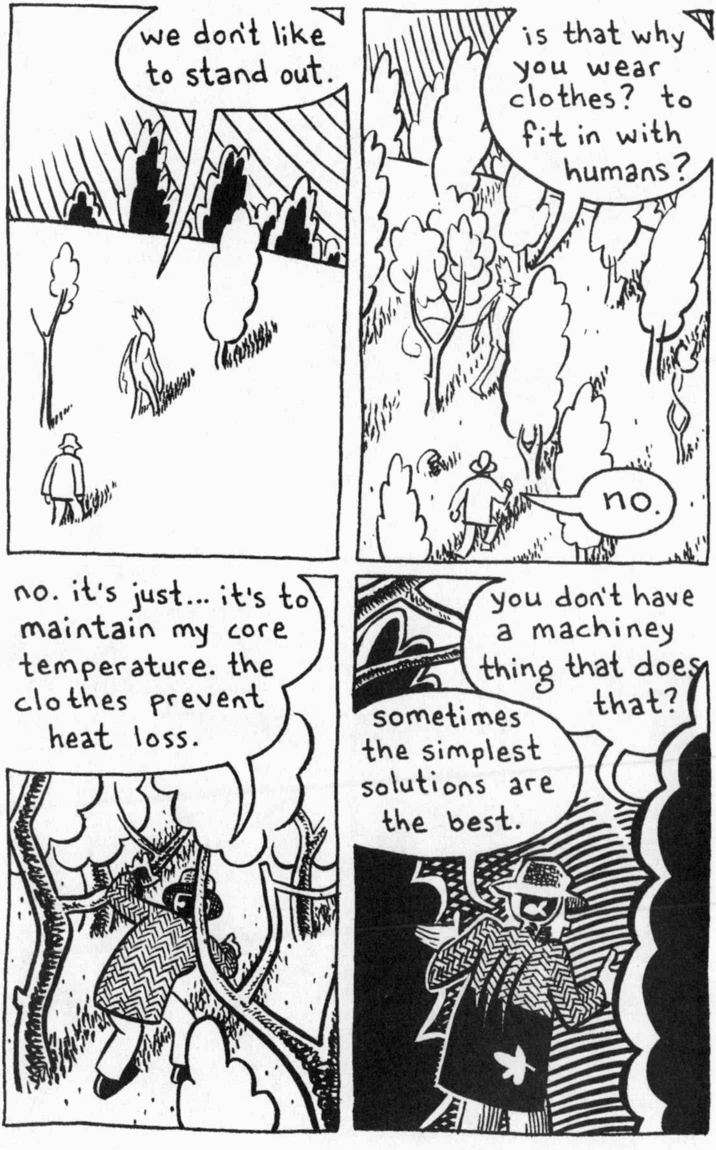
we don't like to stand out.
is that why you wear clothes? to fit in with humans?
no.
no. it's just... it's to maintain my core temperature. the clothes prevent heat loss.
you don't have a machiney thing that does that?
sometimes the simplest solutions are the best.

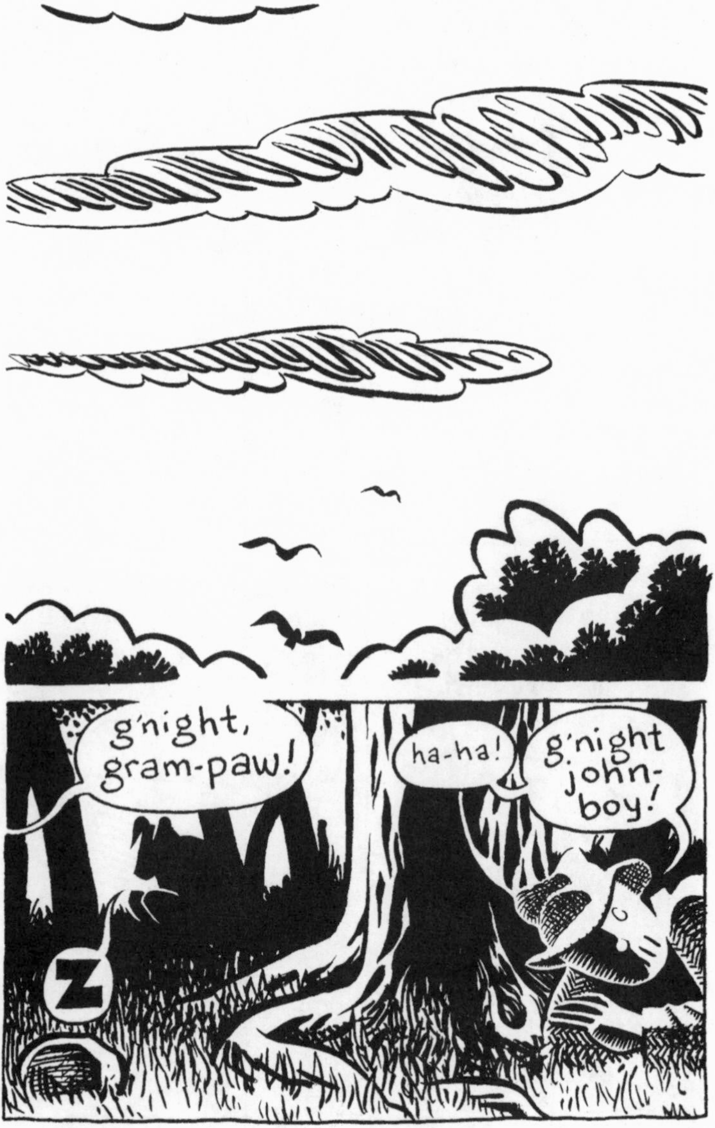
g'night, gram-paw!
ha-ha!
g'night john-boy!
z

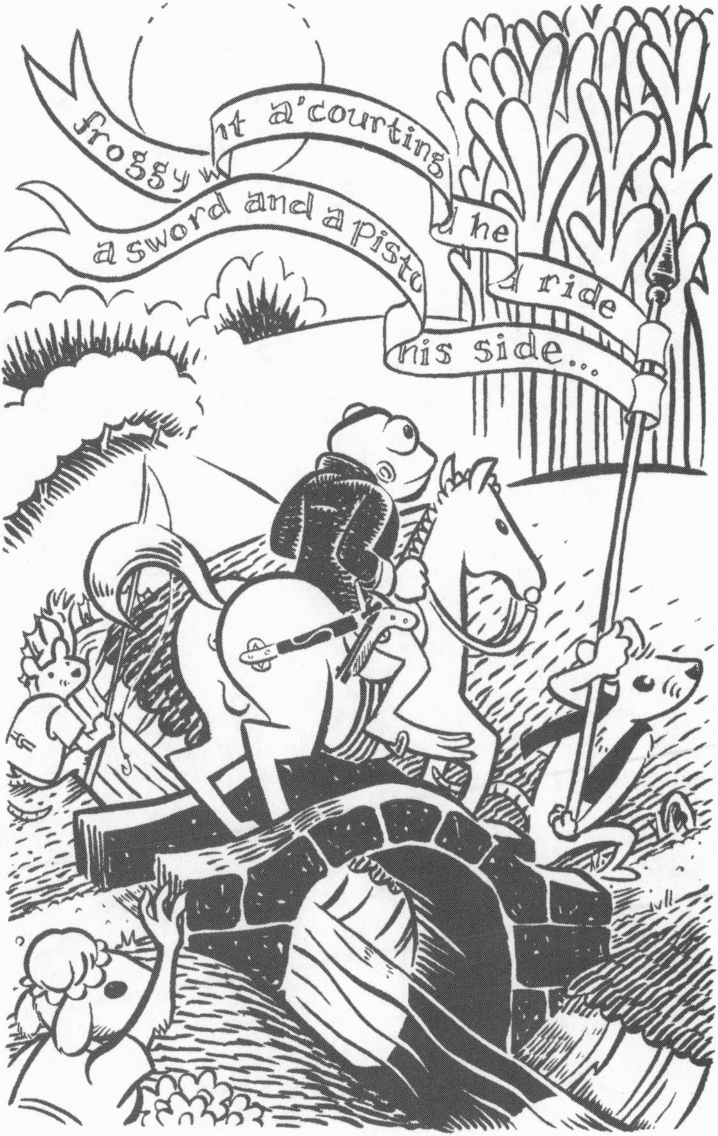
froggy w
nt a'courting
a sword and a pisto
d he
d ride
nis side...

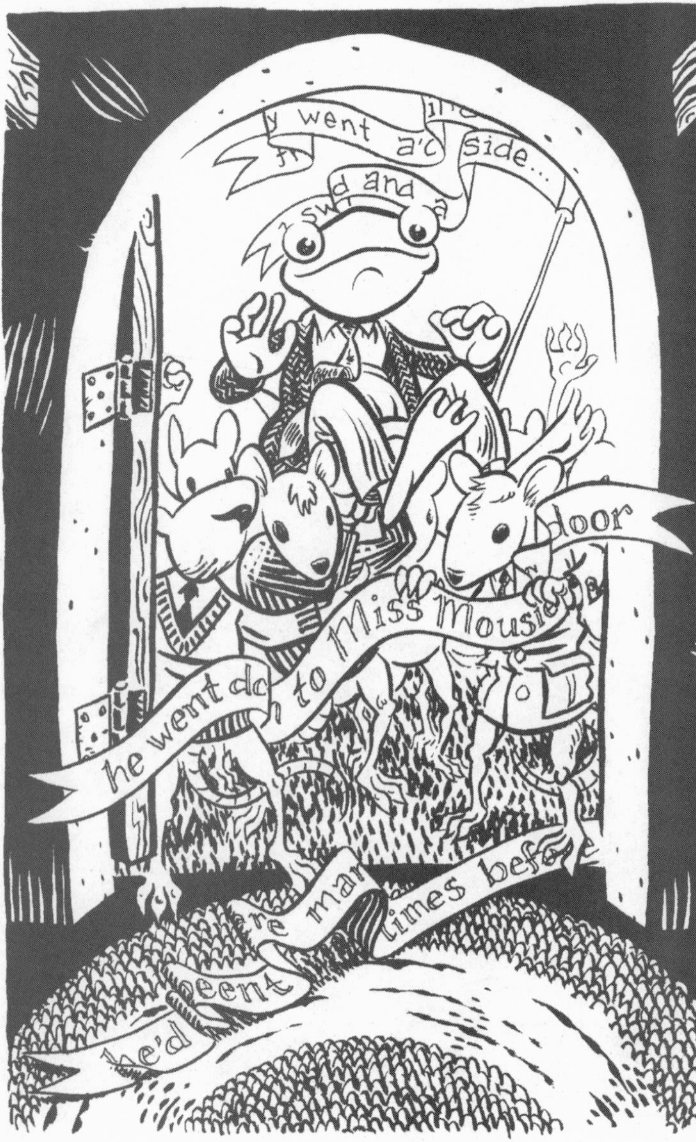

went
side...
and
he went
to Miss Mousie
door
he'd
times

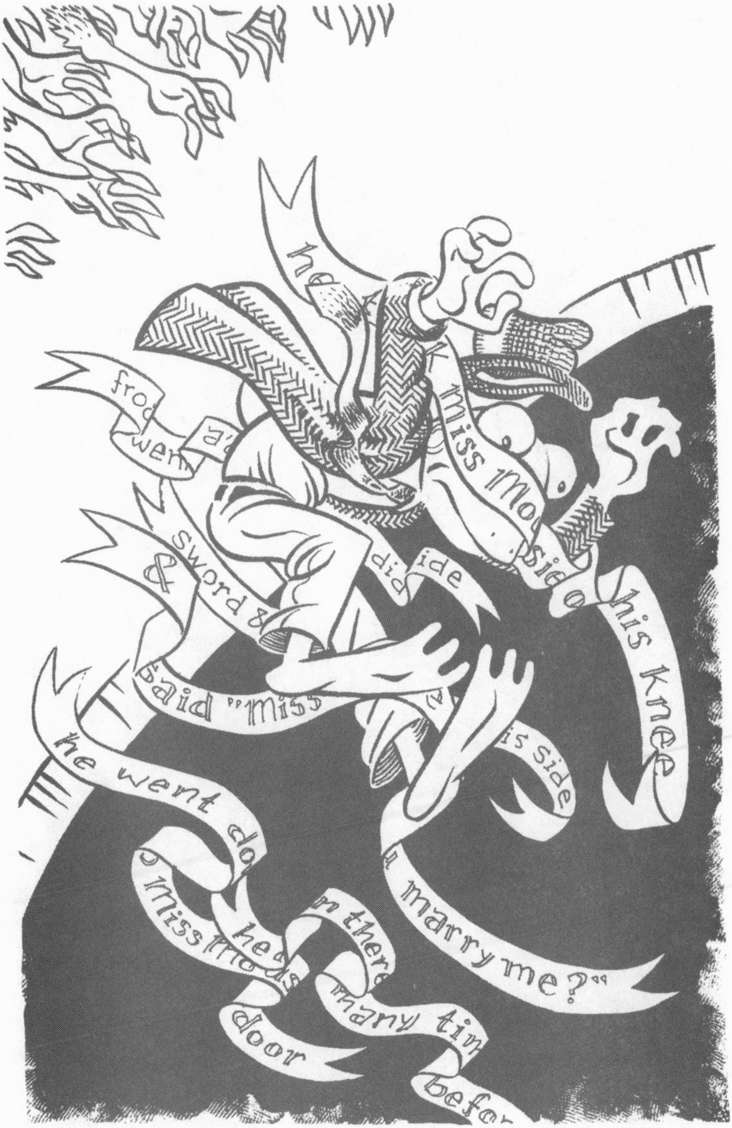
he
frog
went
Miss Mo
sword &
&
did
side
side o
his Knee
said "Miss
is side
he went do
Miss Mo
he
n there
marry me?"
door
many tim
befor

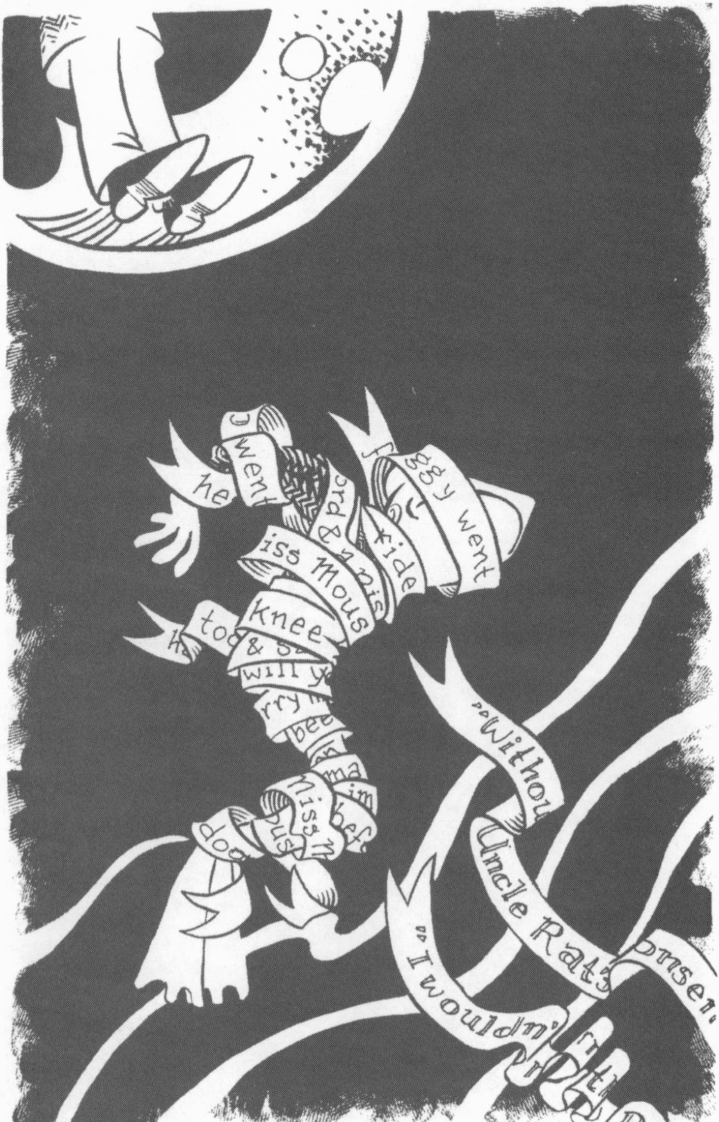

he
went
iss Mous
knee
will y
went
"Withou
Uncle Rat's
onsent
"I wouldn't

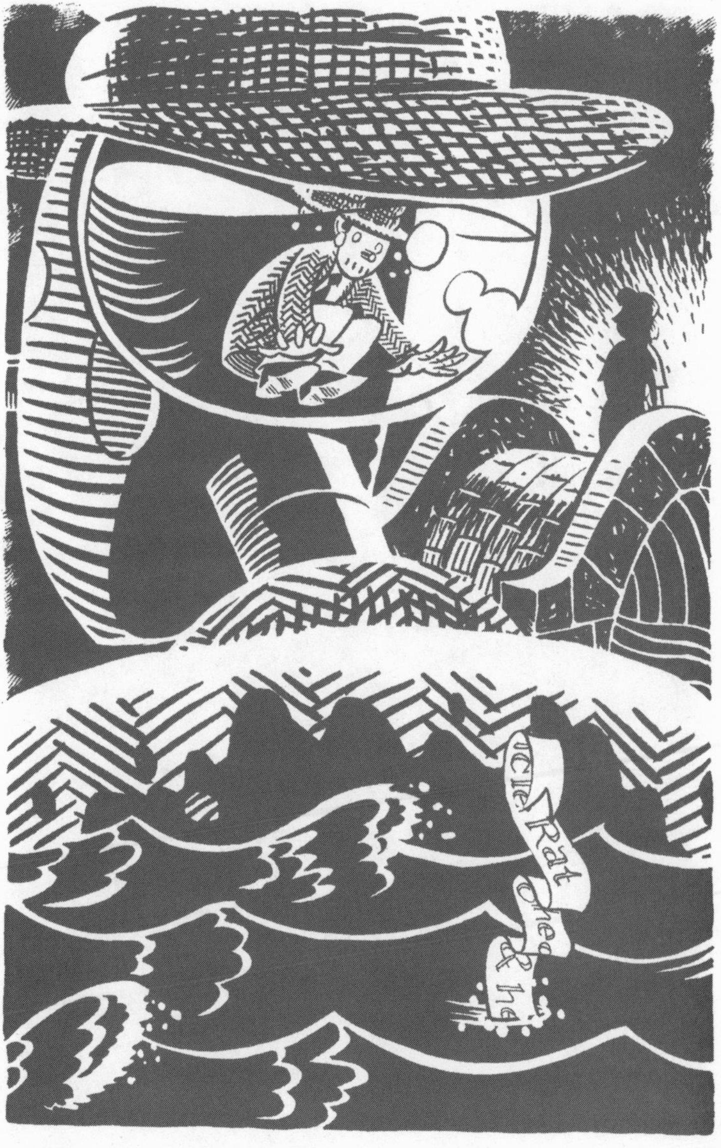
Rat

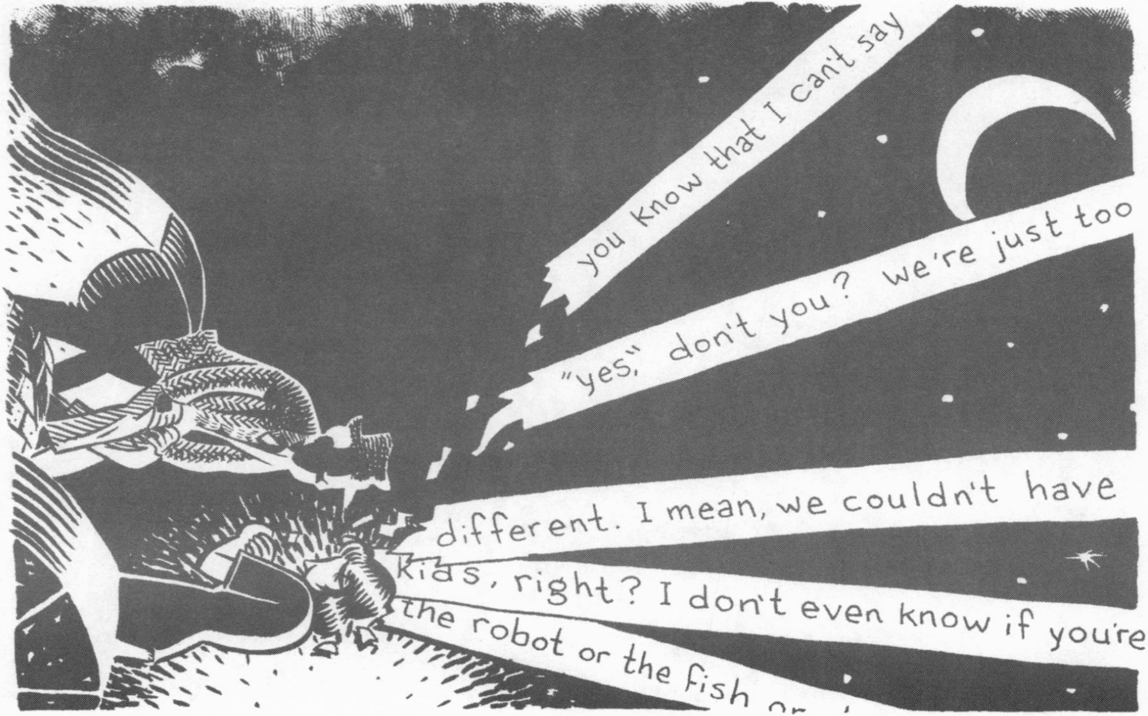
you know that I can't say
"yes," don't you? we're just too
different. I mean, we couldn't have
kids, right? I don't even know if you're
the robot or the fish

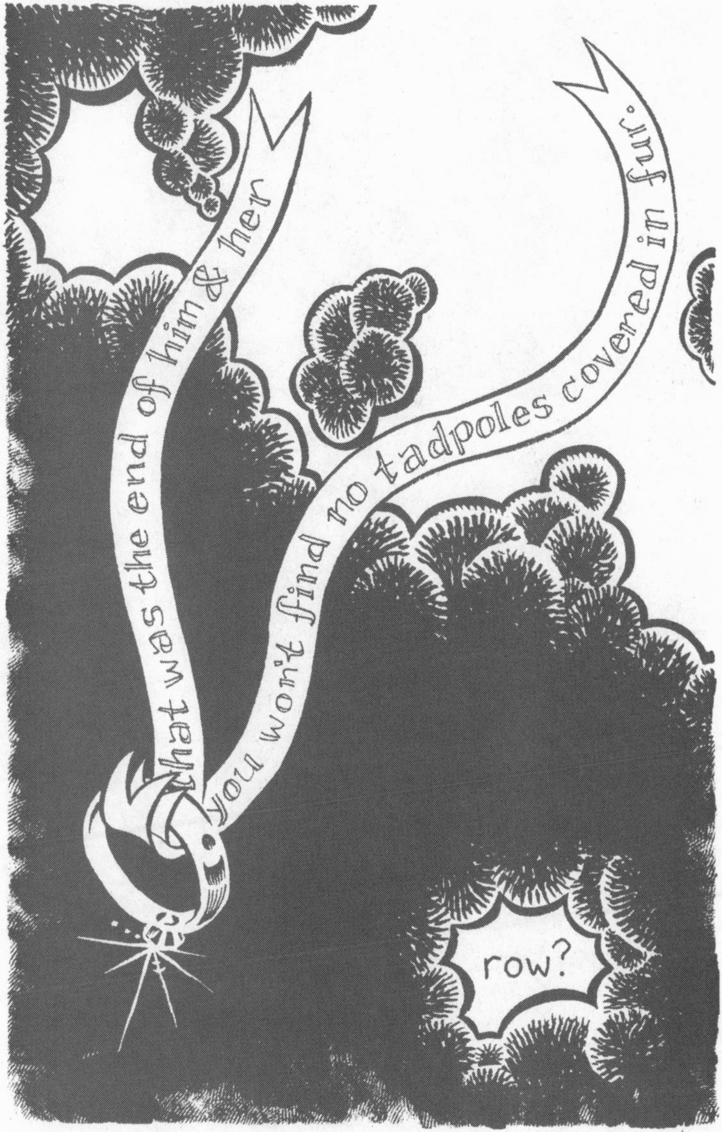
that was the end of him & her
you won't find no tadpoles covered in fur.
row?

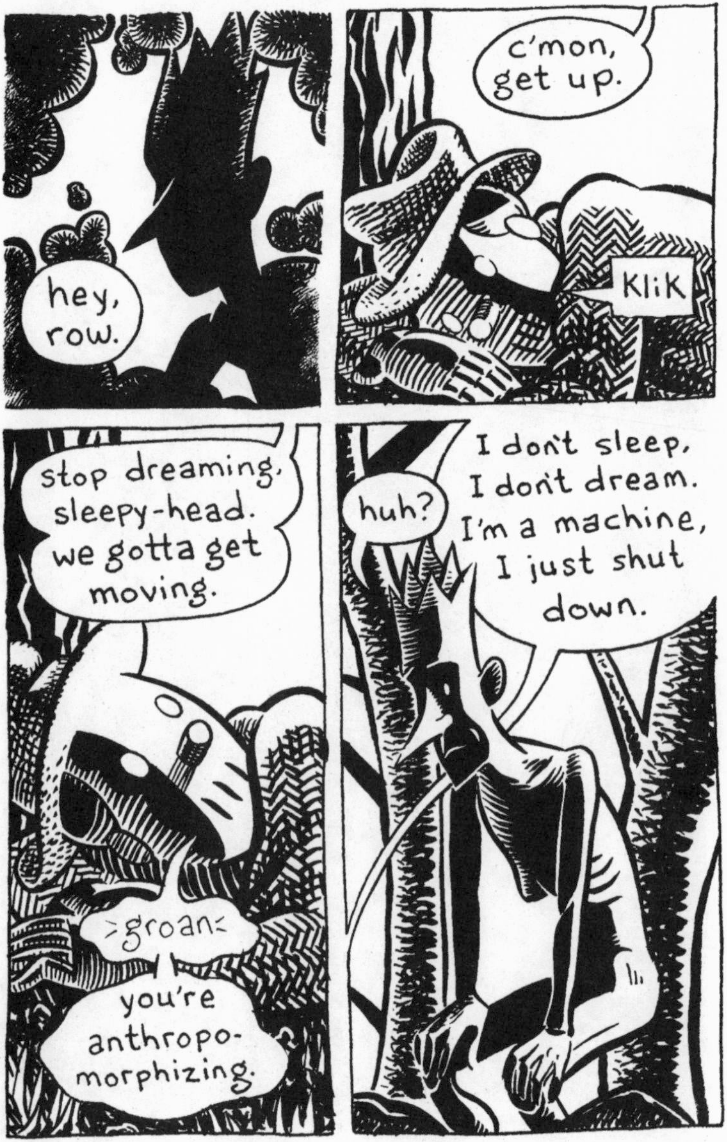
hey, row.
c'mon, get up.
KliK
stop dreaming, sleepy-head. we gotta get moving.
>groan<
you're anthropo-morphizing.
huh?
I don't sleep, I don't dream. I'm a machine, I just shut down.

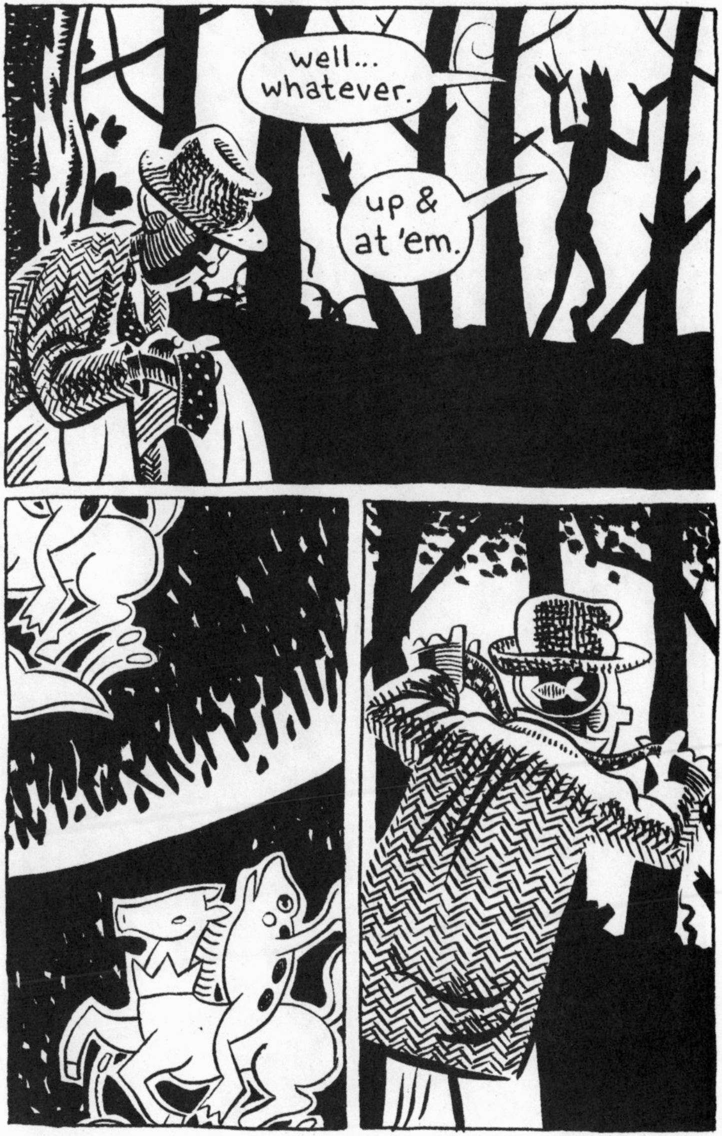
well... whatever.
up & at 'em.

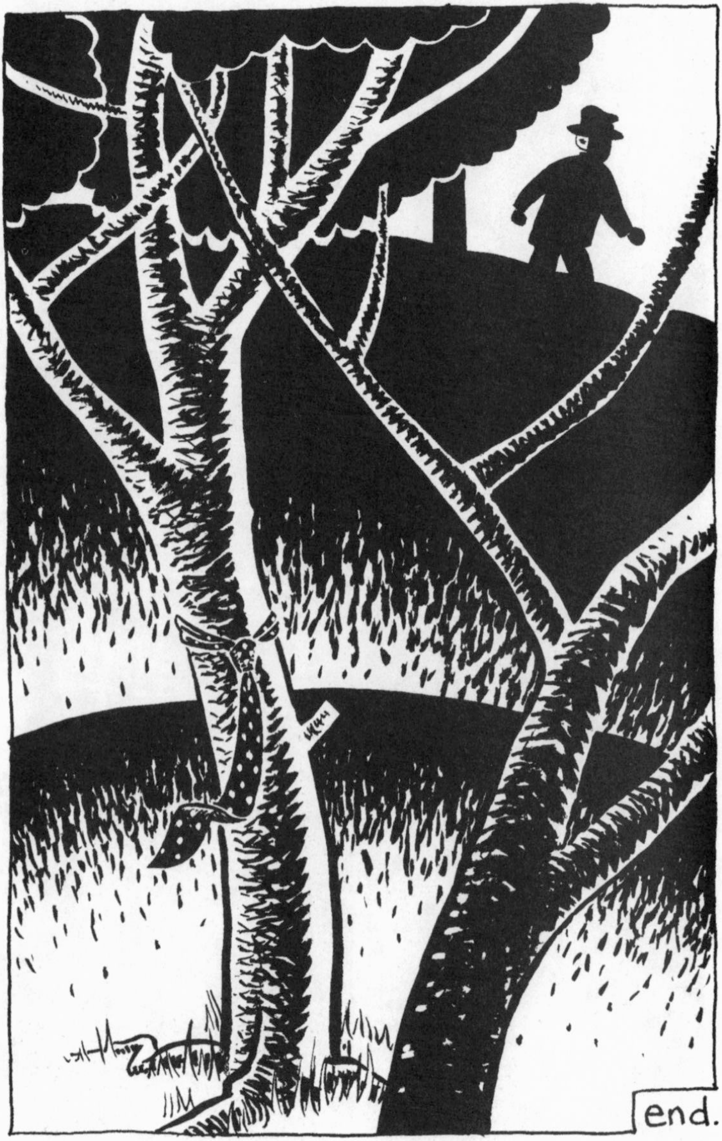
end.

rowbot, bull, & delaware thistle

in

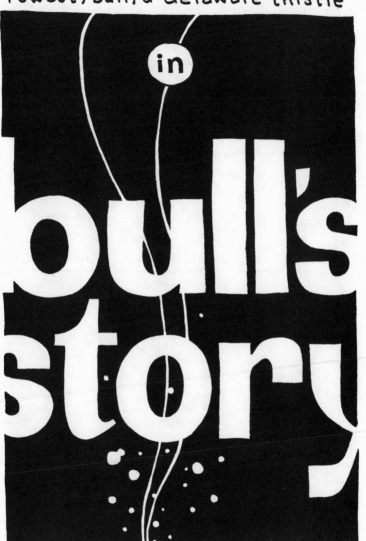

bull's
story

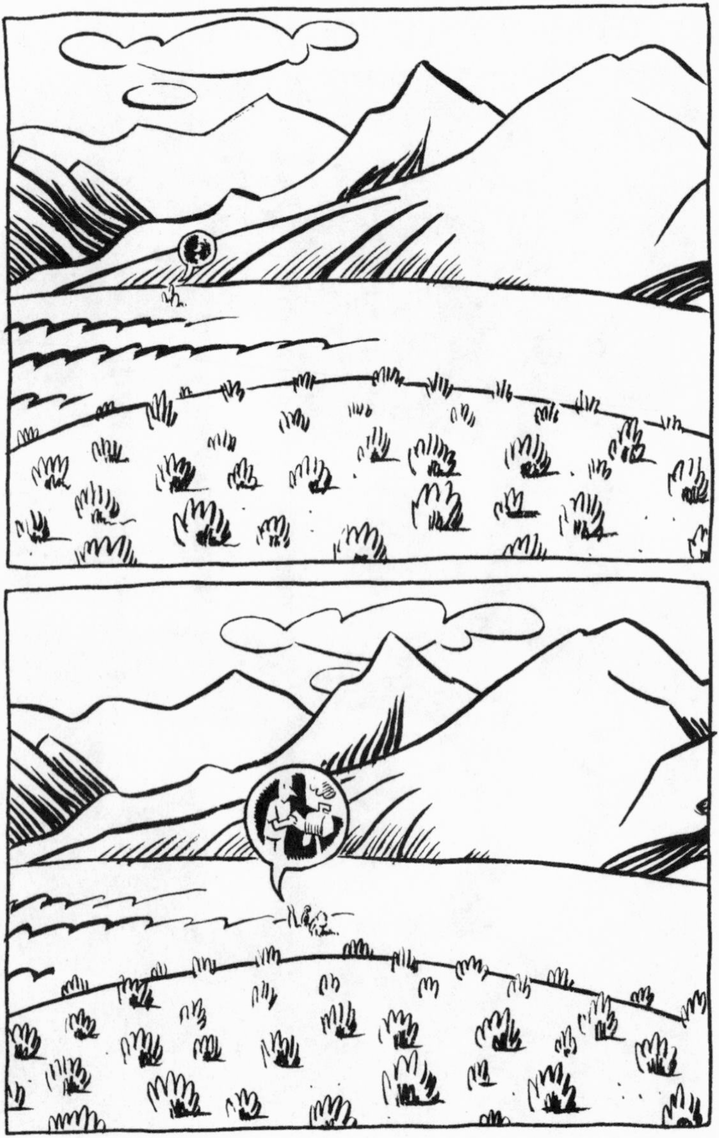

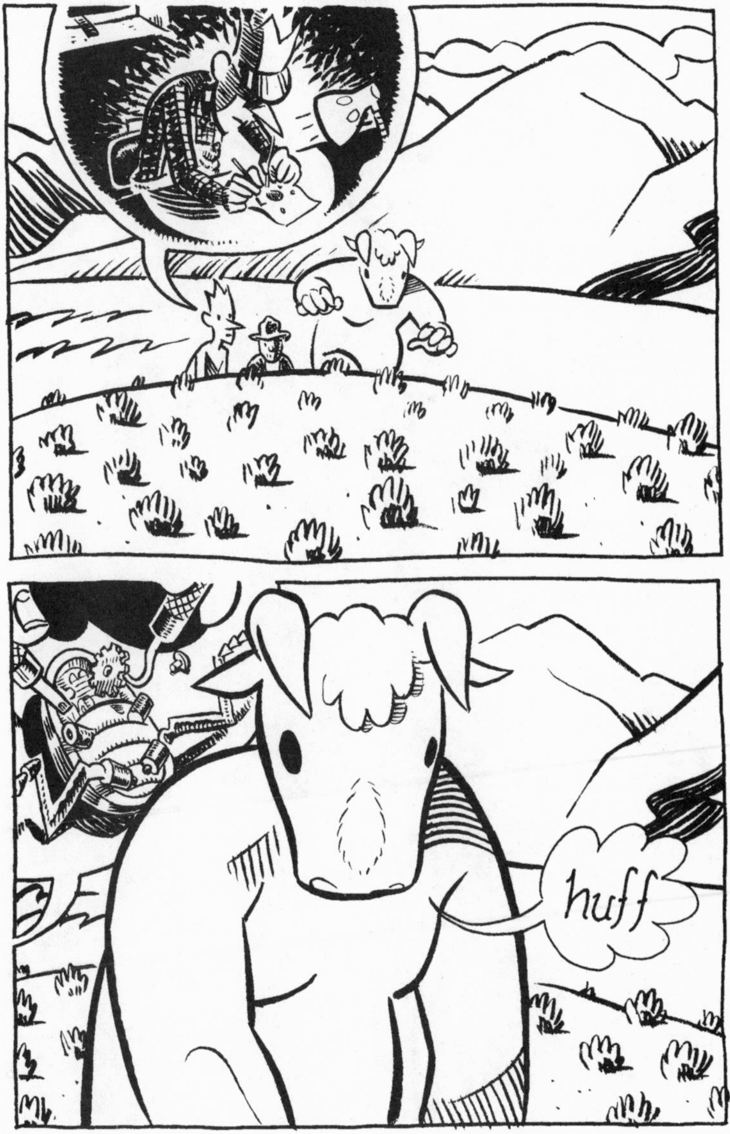
huff

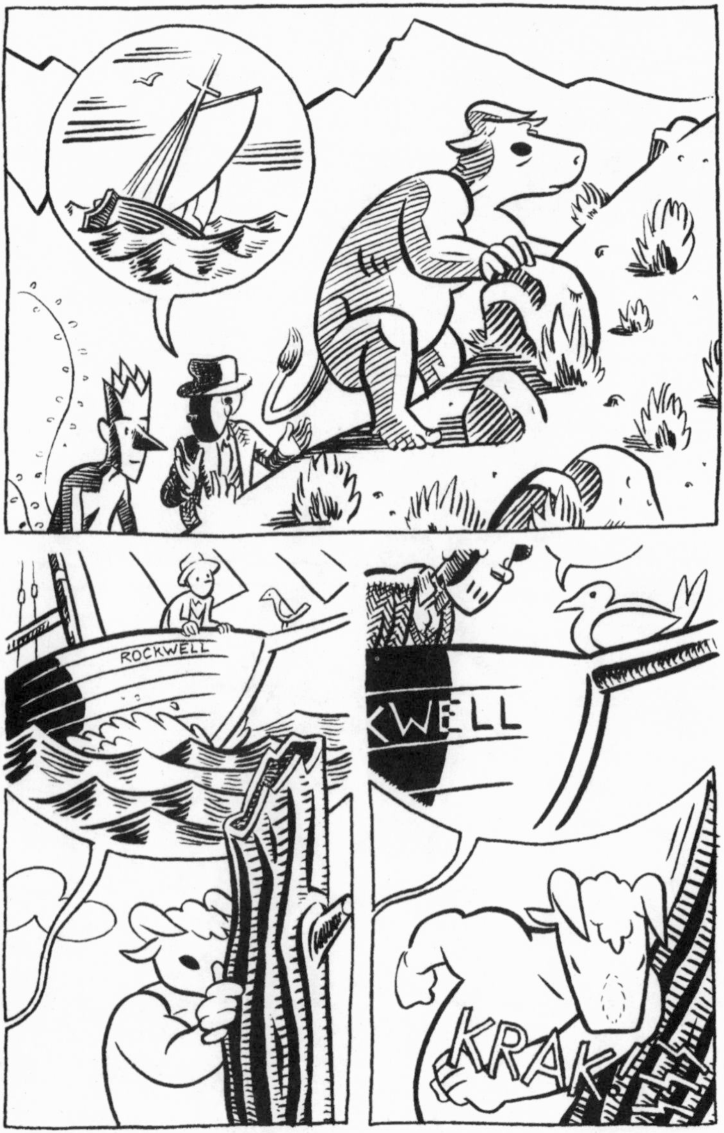
ROCKWELL
KWELL
KRAK

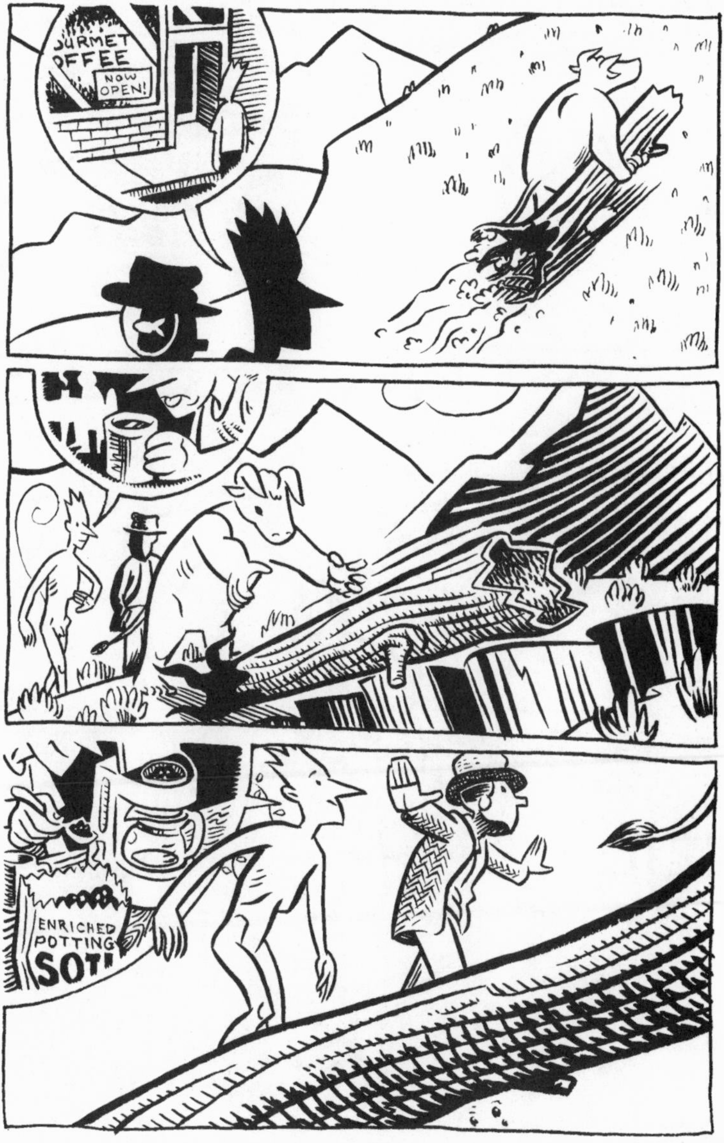
NOW OPEN!
ENRICHED
POTTING

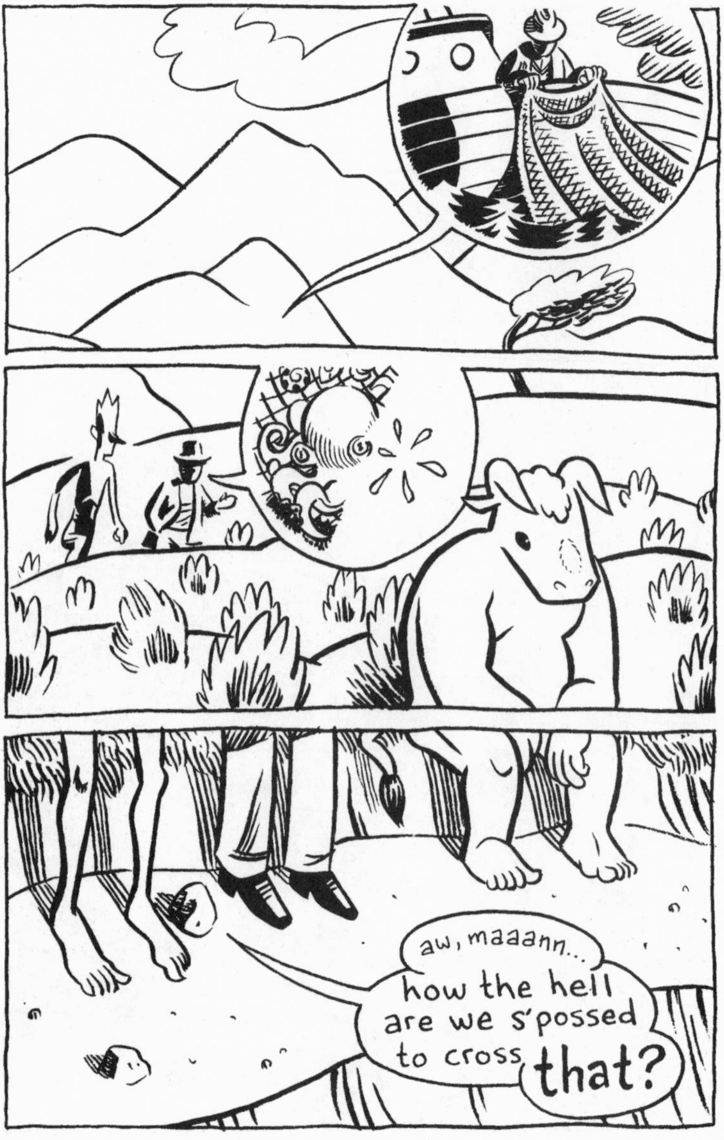
aw, maaann...
how the hell are we s'possed to cross that?

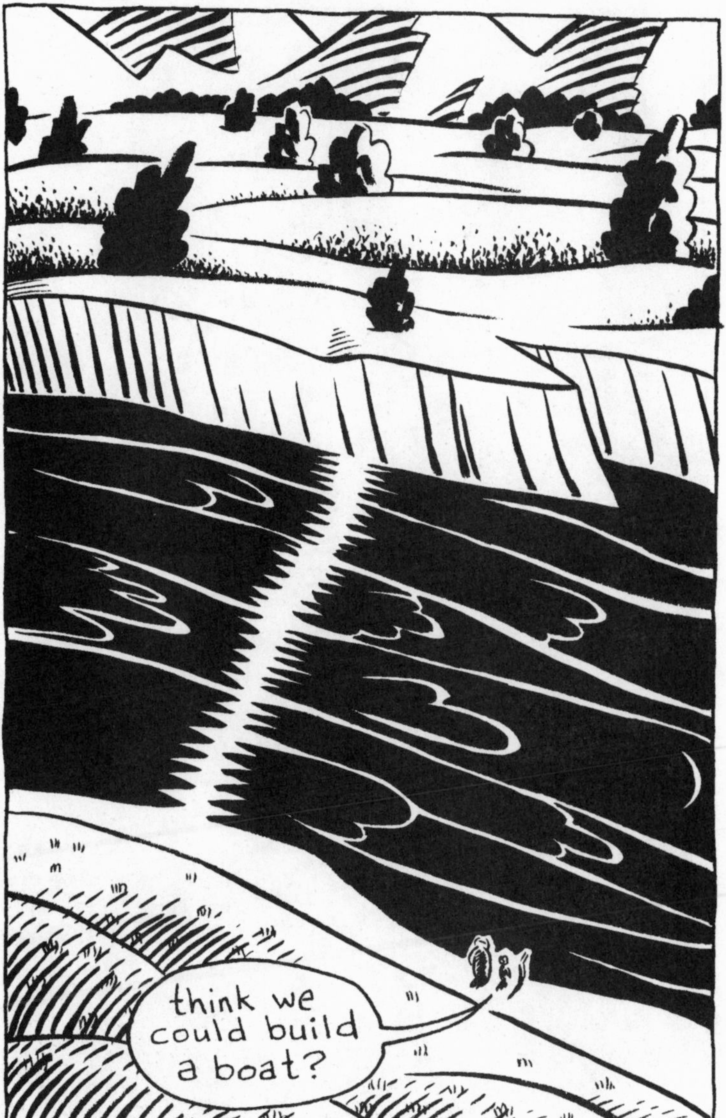
think we could build a boat?

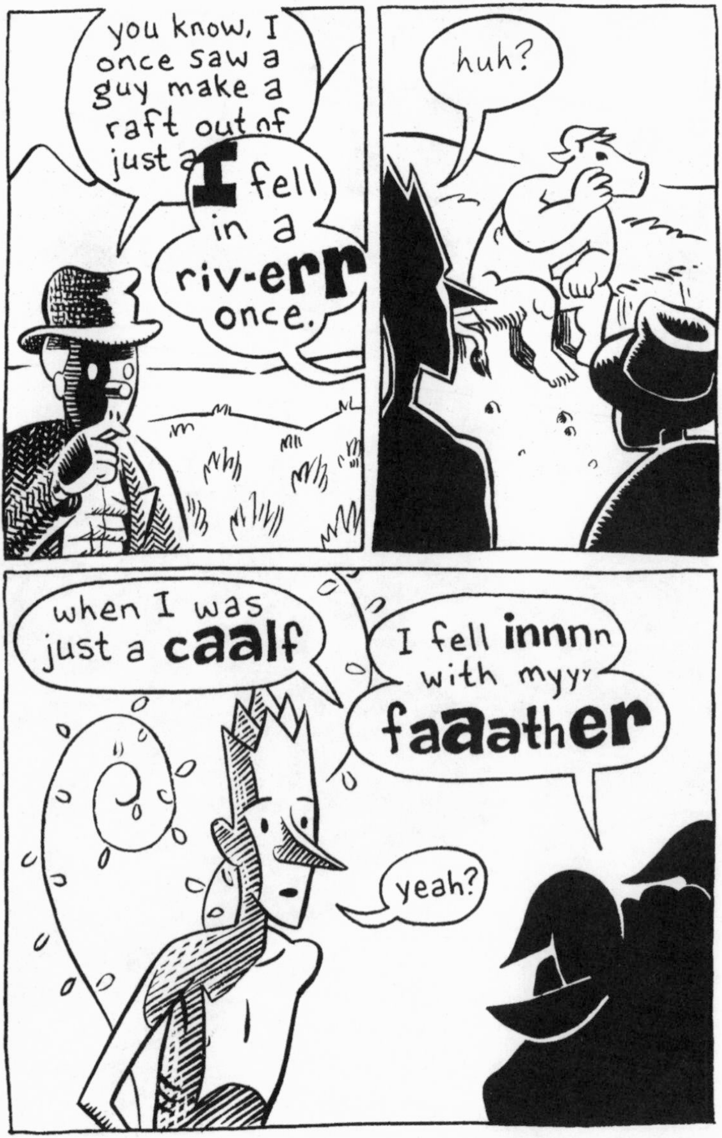

you know, I once saw a guy make a raft out of just a
I fell in a riv-err once.
huh?
when I was just a caaalf
I fell innnn with myyy faaather
yeah?

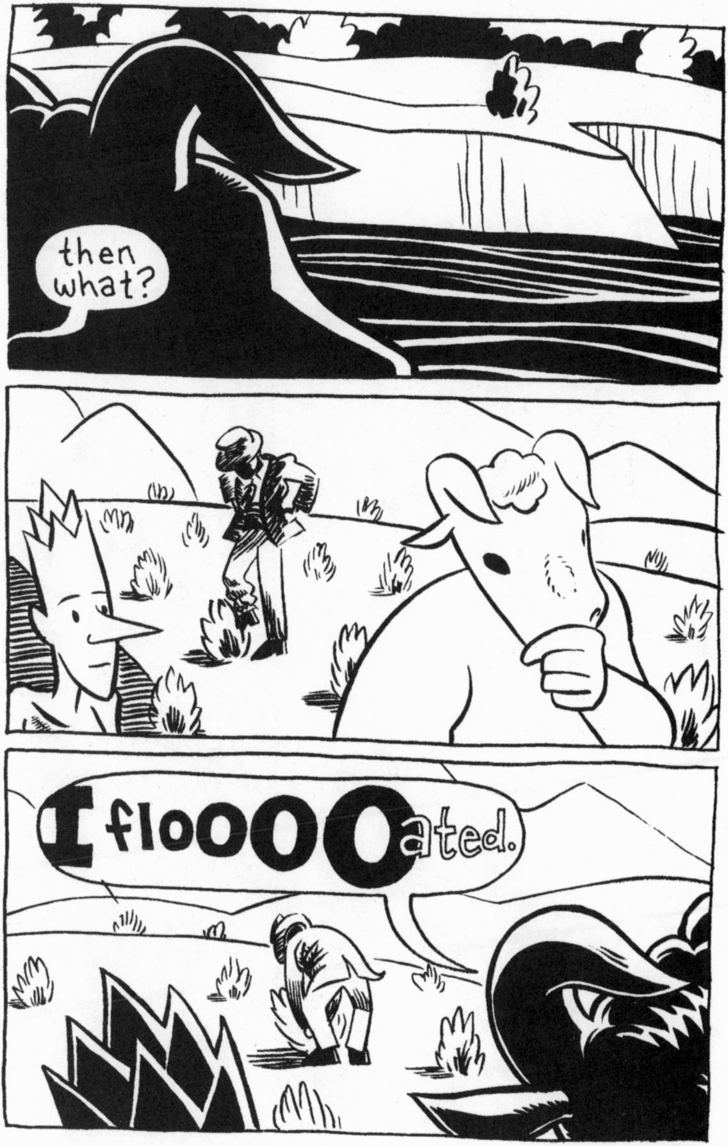
then what?
I flooOOOated.

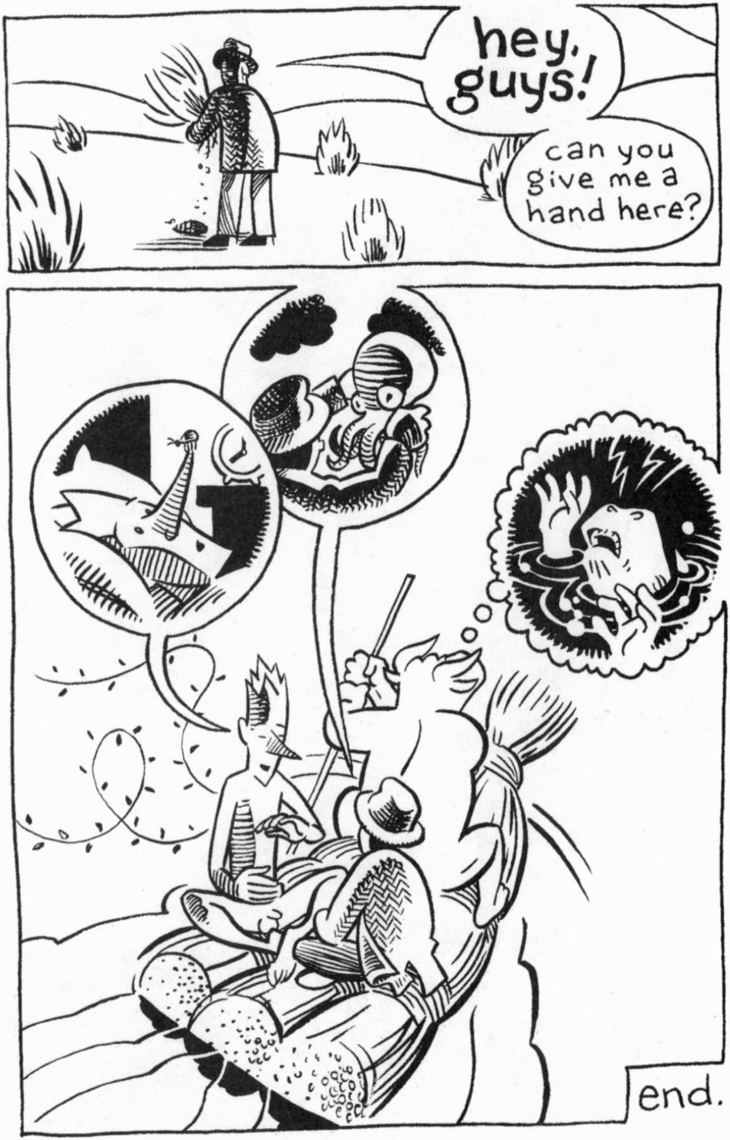
hey, guys!
can you give me a hand here?
end.

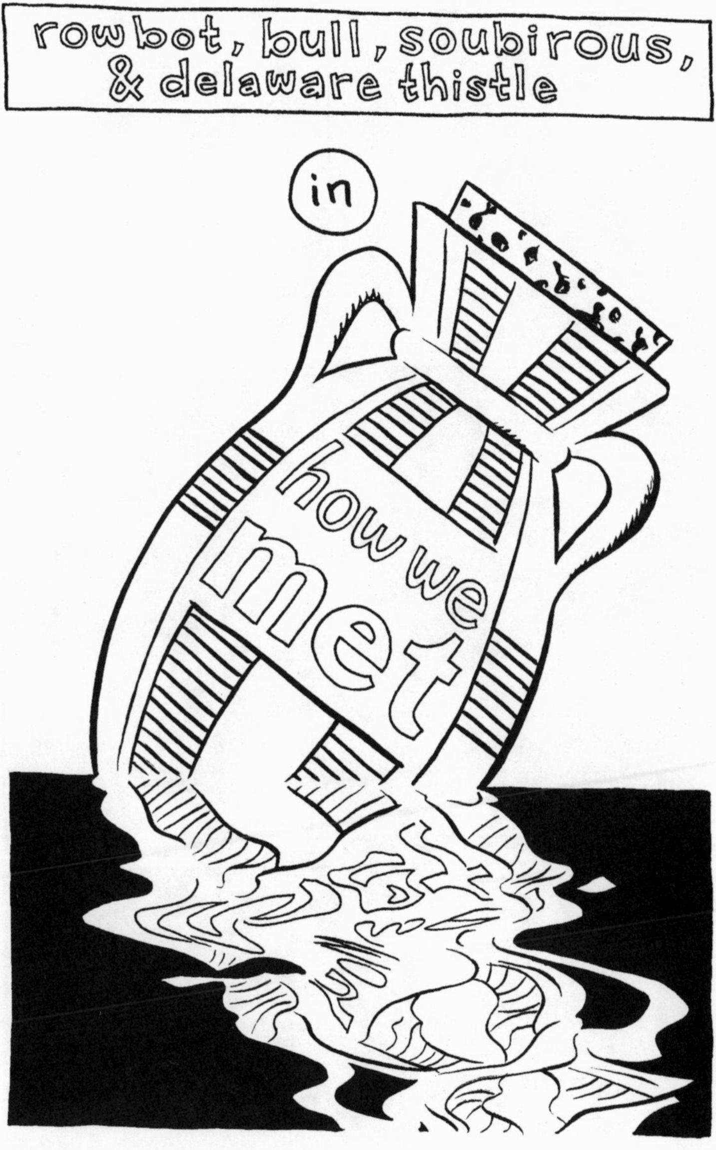
rowbot, bull, soubirous, & delaware thistle
in
how we met

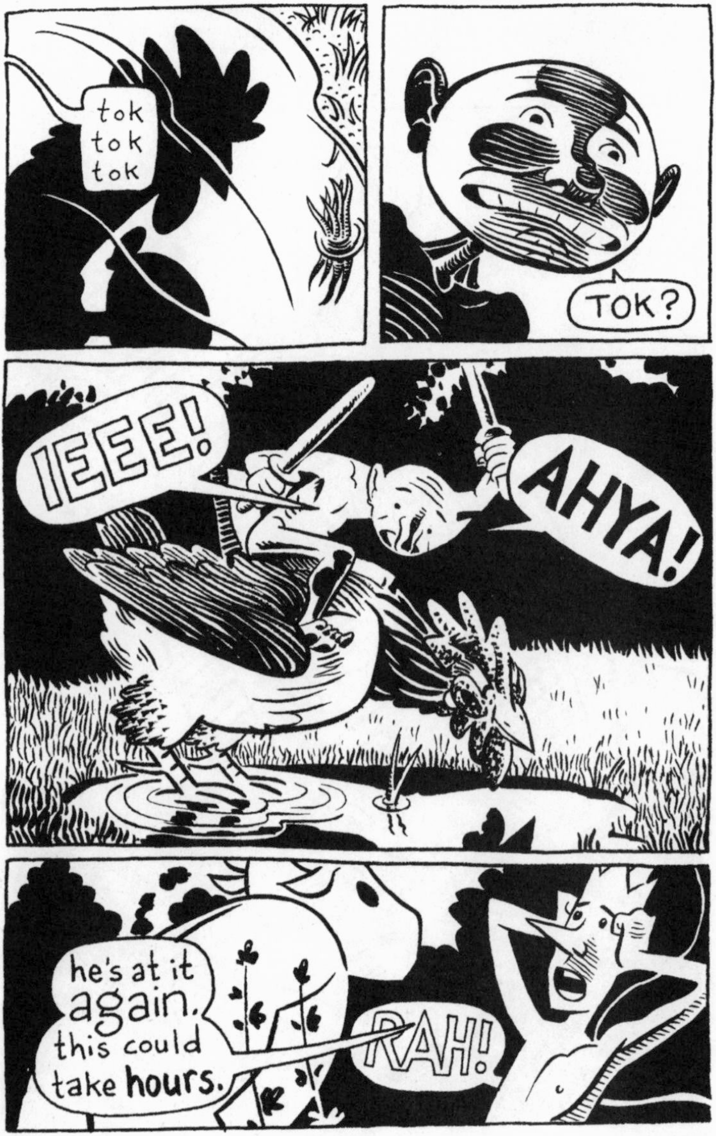
tok
tok
tok
TOK?
IEEE!
AHYA!
he's at it again. this could take **hours**.
RAH!

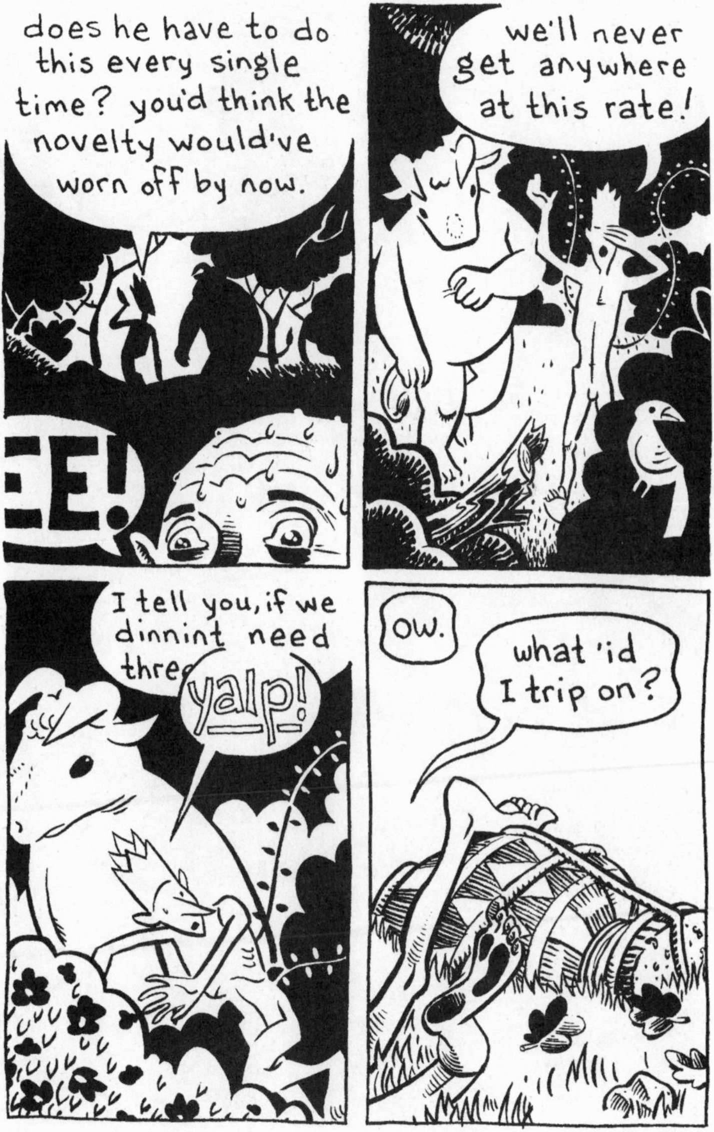
does he have to do this every single time? you'd think the novelty would've worn off by now.
EE!
we'll never get anywhere at this rate!
I tell you, if we dinnint need thre
yalp!
ow.
what 'id I trip on?

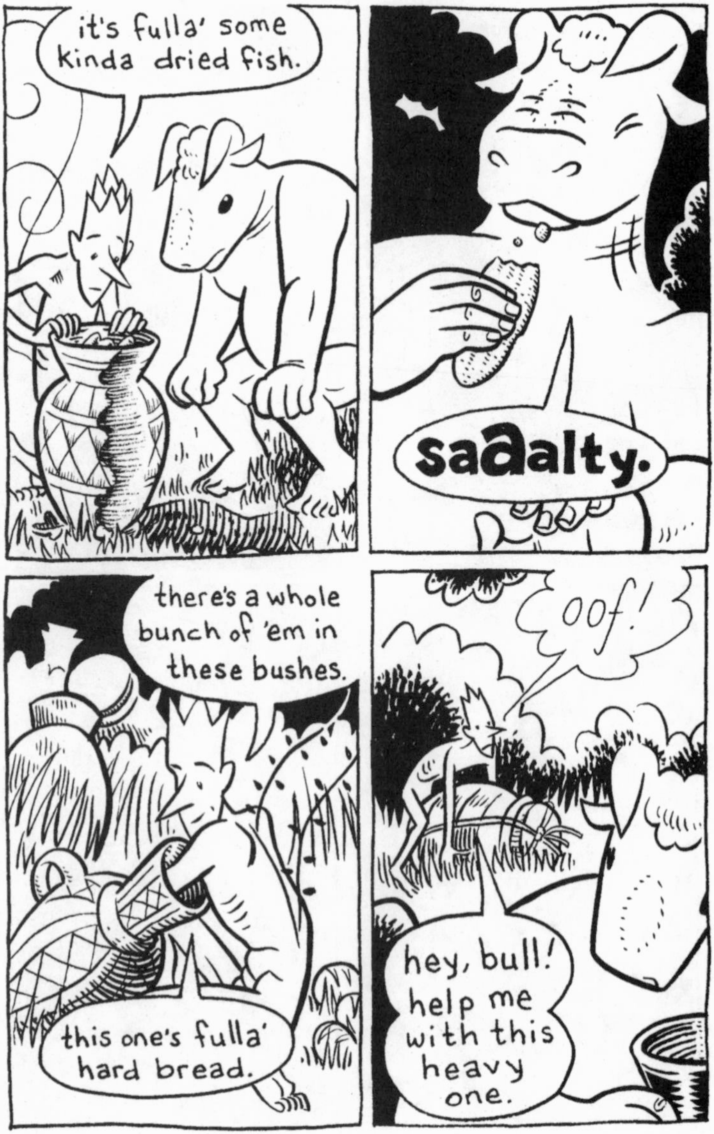
it's fulla' some kinda dried fish.
saaalty.
there's a whole bunch of 'em in these bushes.
this one's fulla' hard bread.
oof!
hey, bull! help me with this heavy one.

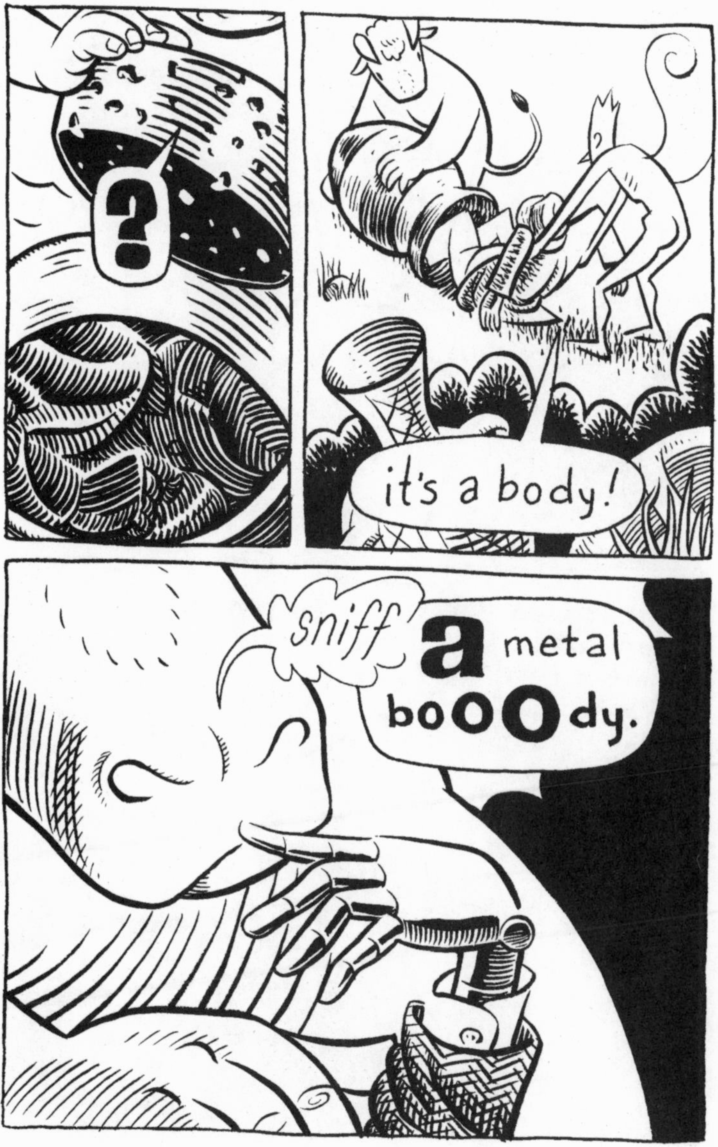
?
it's a body!
sniff
a metal boOOdy.

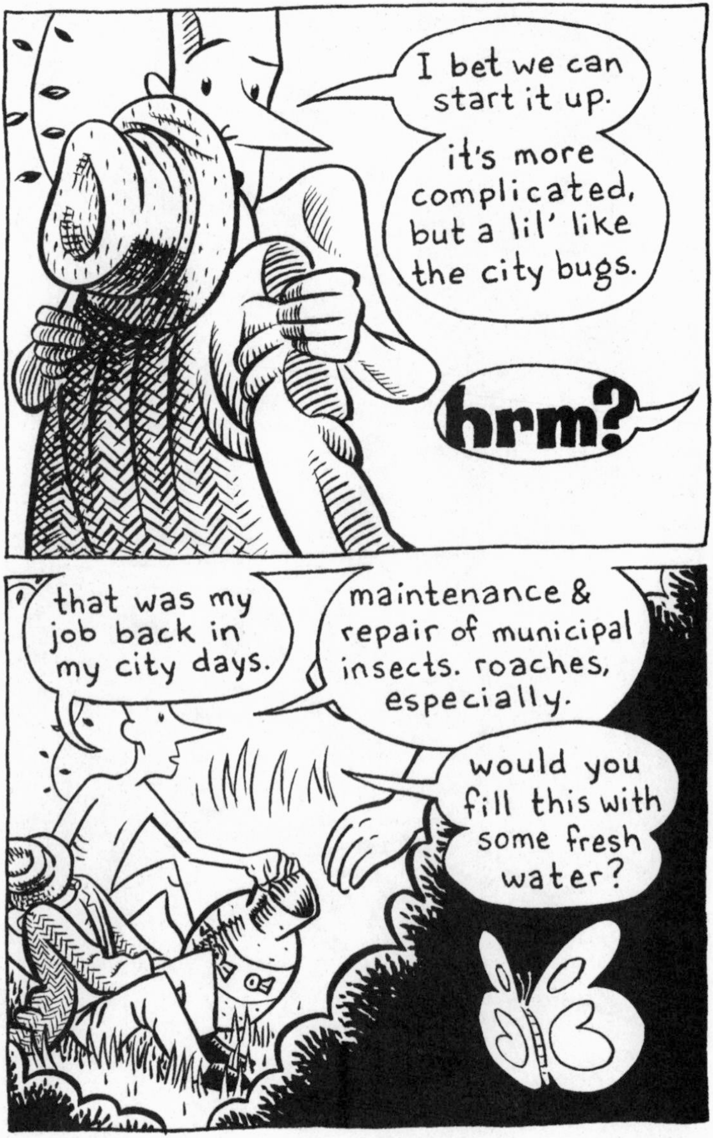
I bet we can start it up.
it's more complicated, but a lil' like the city bugs.
hrm?
that was my job back in my city days.
maintenance & repair of municipal insects. roaches, especially.
would you fill this with some fresh water?

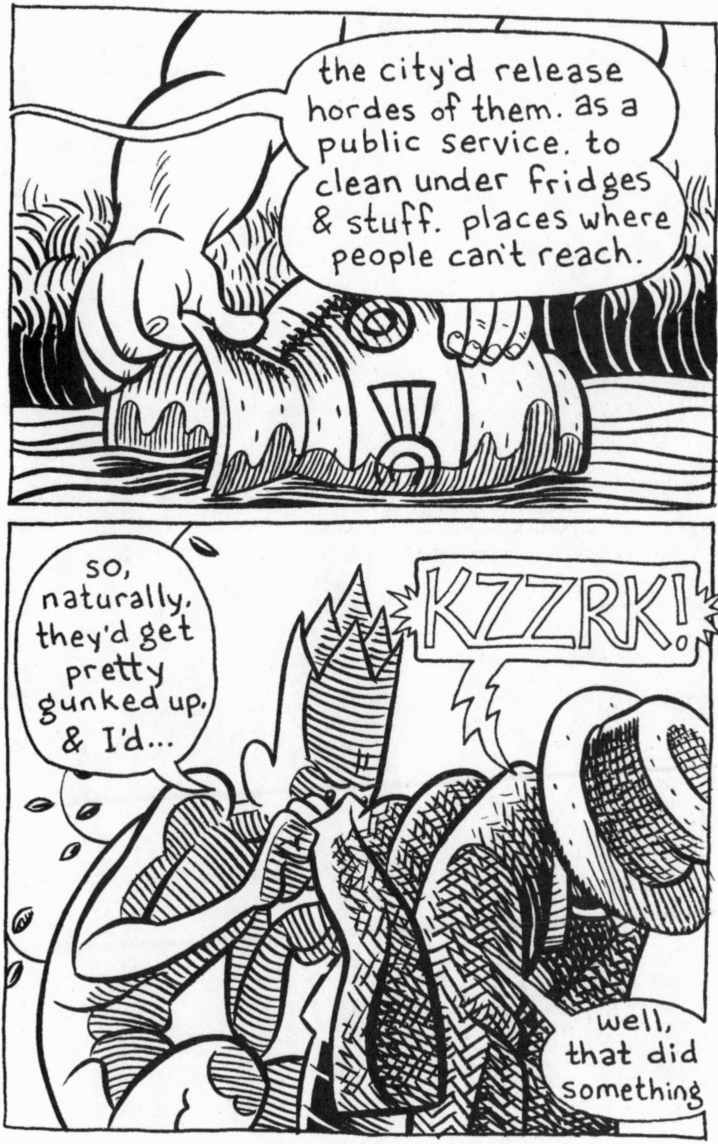
the city'd release hordes of them. as a public service. to clean under fridges & stuff. places where people can't reach.
so, naturally, they'd get pretty gunked up, & I'd...
KZZRK!
well, that did something

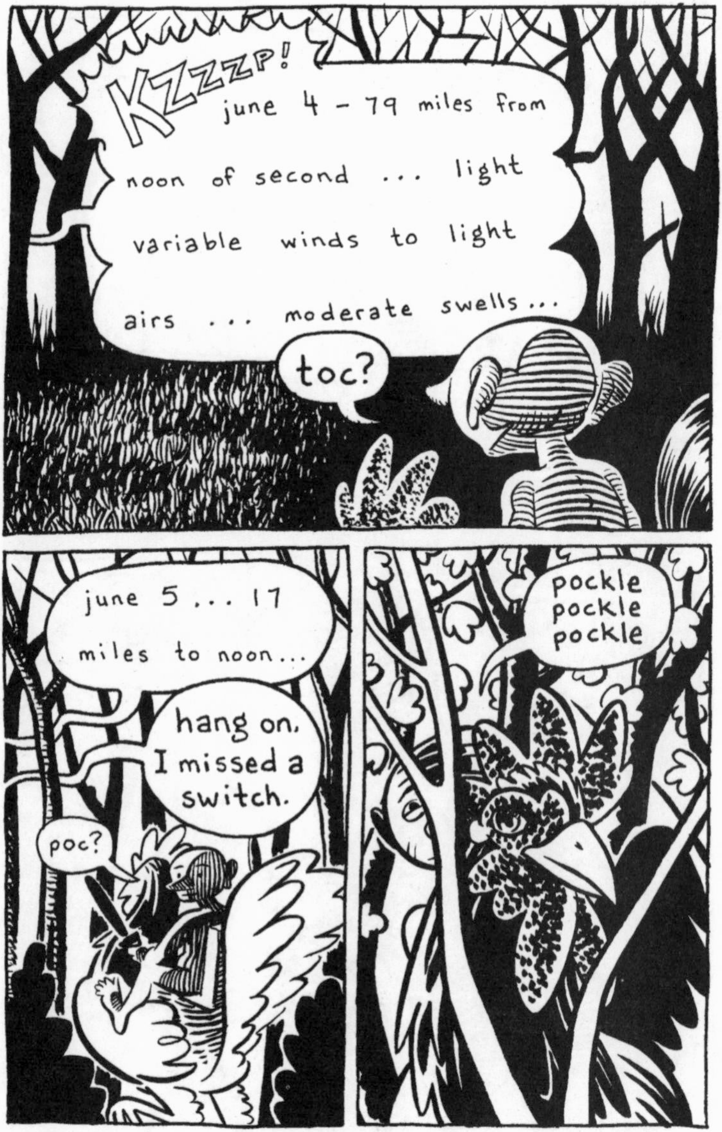
KZZZZP!
june 4 - 79 miles from noon of second ... light variable winds to light airs ... moderate swells...
toc?
june 5 ... 17 miles to noon...
hang on. I missed a switch.
poc?
pockle pockle pockle

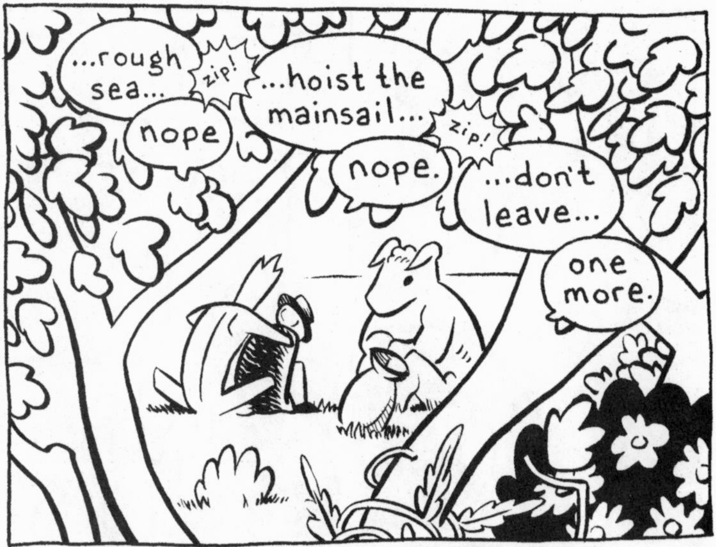
...rough sea...
zip!
nope
...hoist the mainsail...
zip!
nope.
...don't leave...
one more.

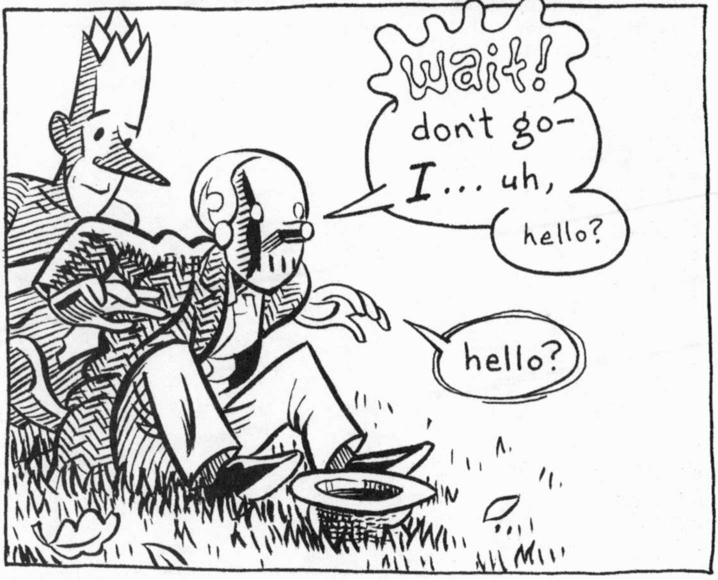
wait! don't go-
I... uh,
hello?
hello?

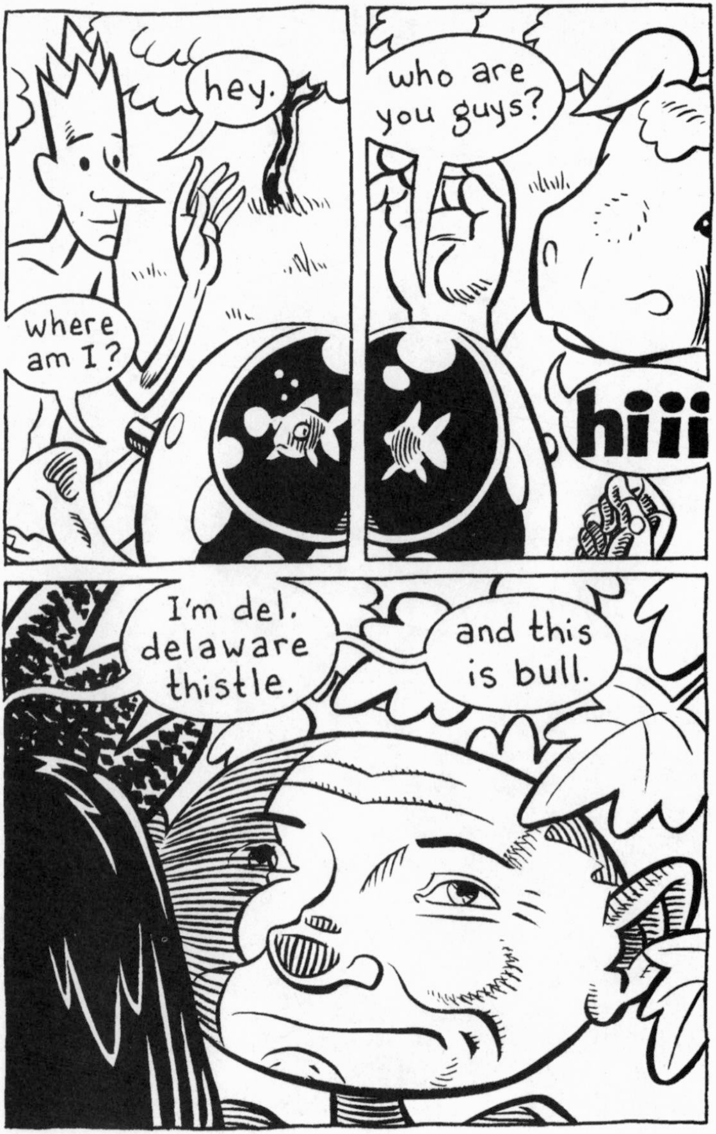
hey.
where am I?
who are you guys?
hiii
I'm del. delaware thistle.
and this is bull.

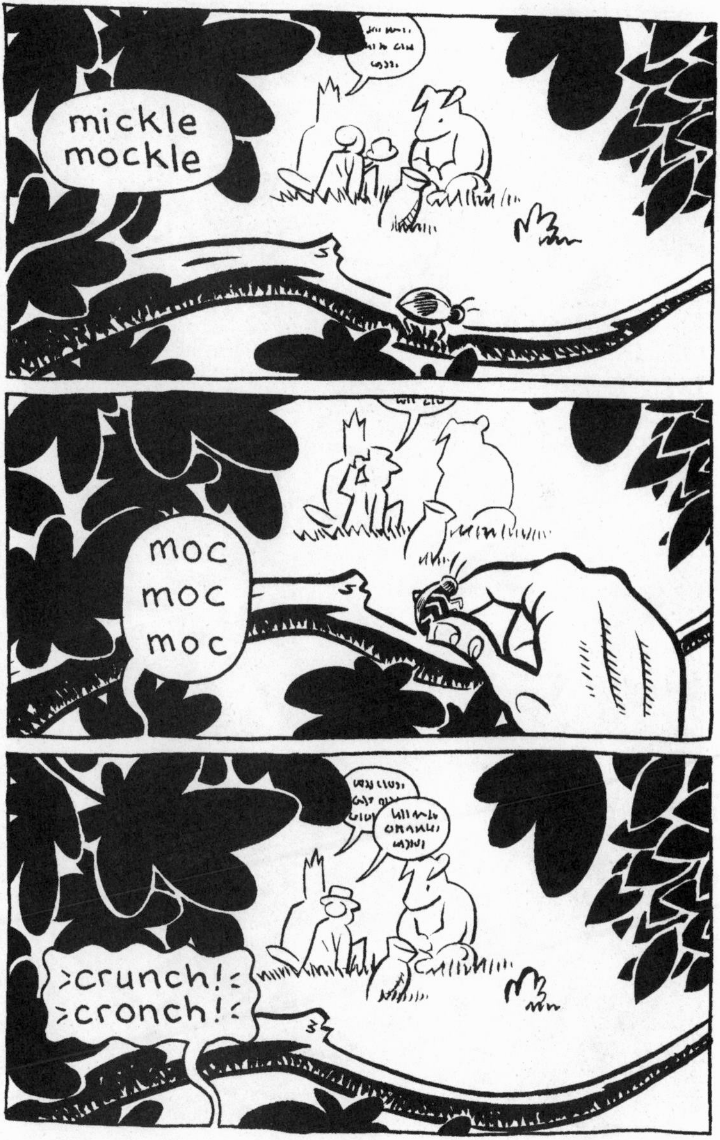
mickle mockle
moc moc moc
>crunch!< >cronch!<

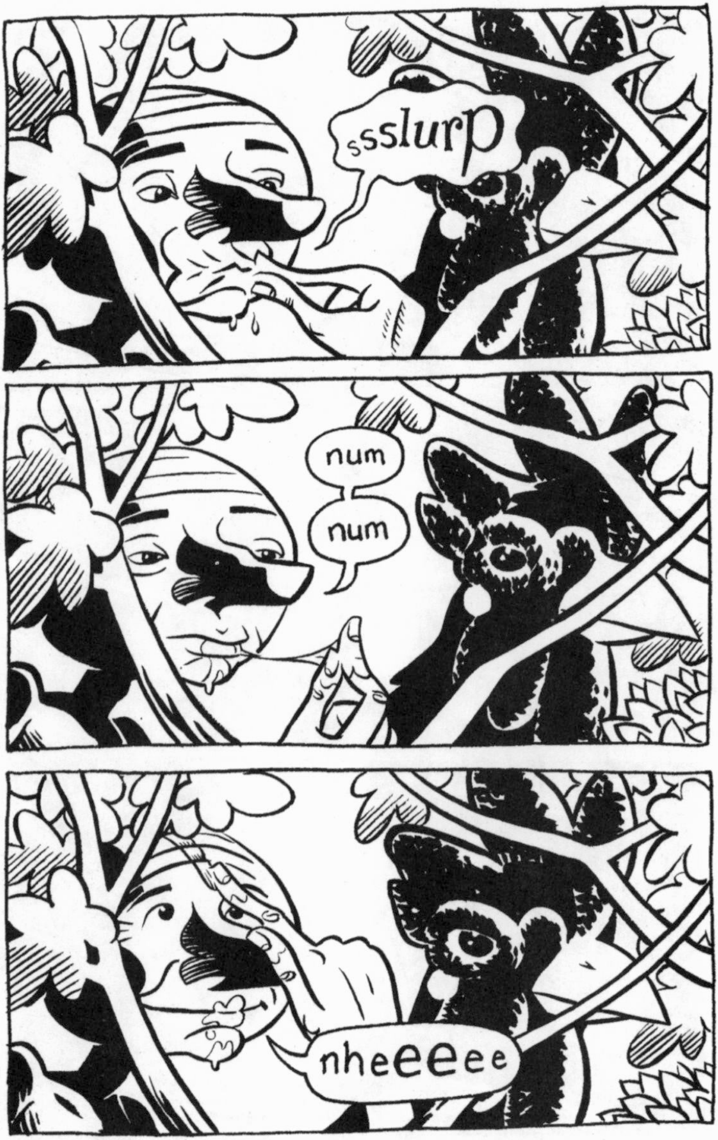
ssslurp
num
num
nheeeeee

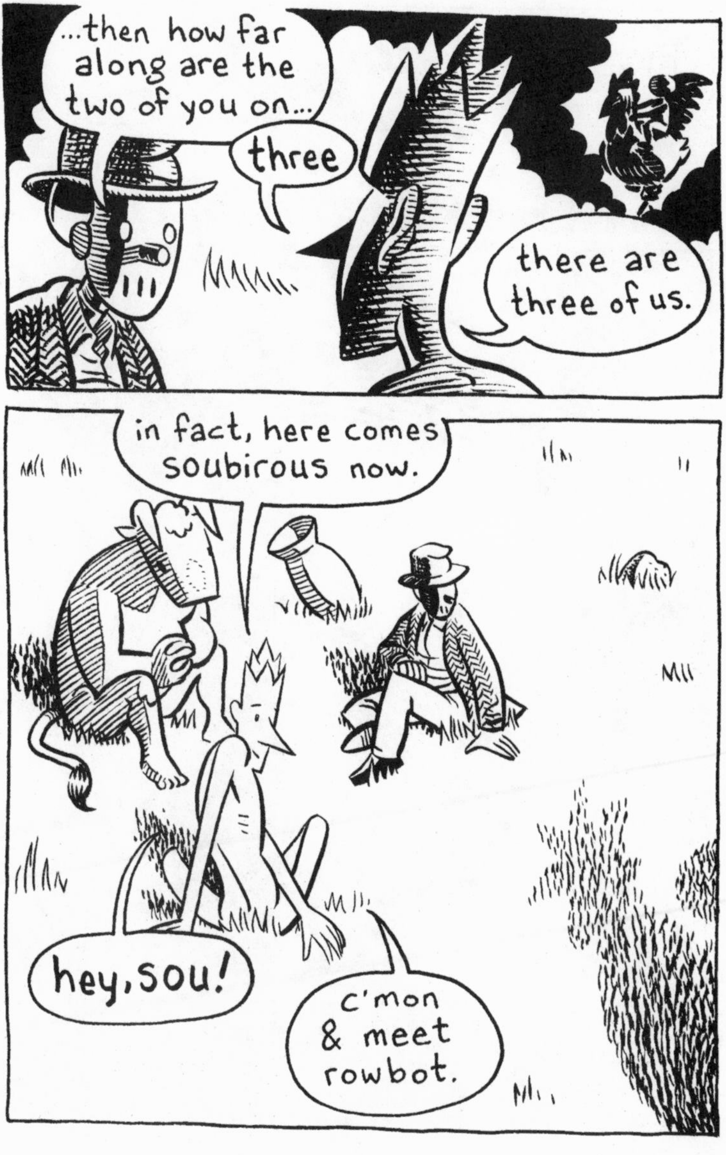
...then how far along are the two of you on...
three
there are three of us.
in fact, here comes soubirous now.
hey, sou!
c'mon & meet rowbot.

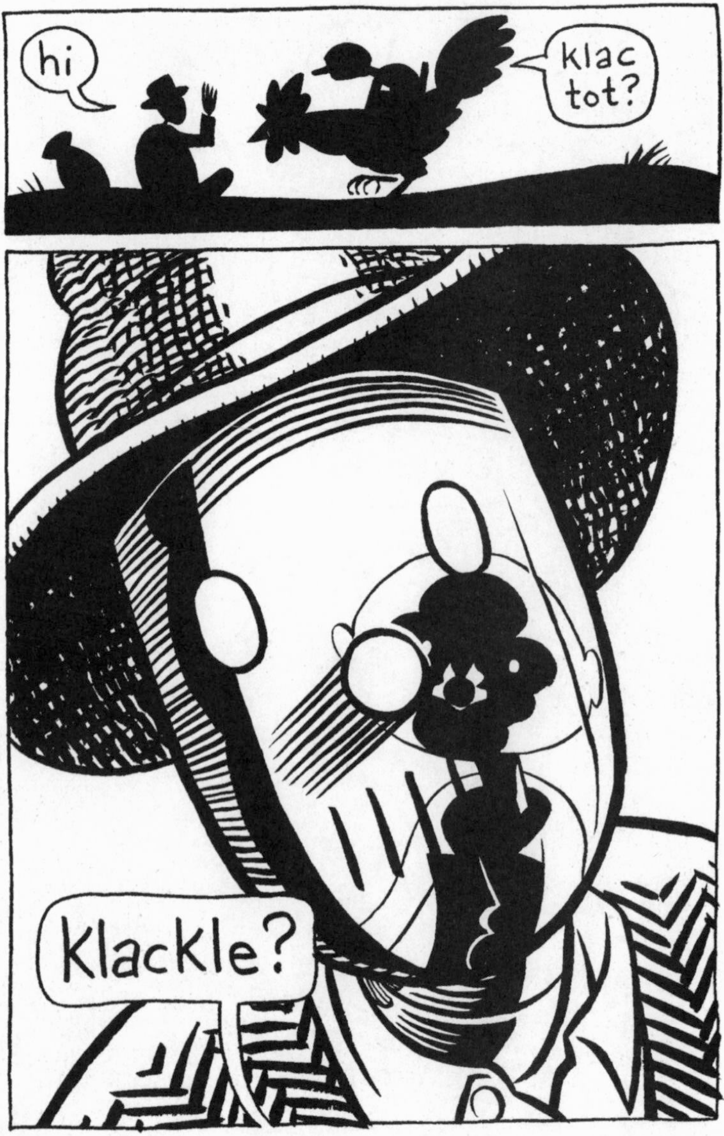
hi
klac tot?
Klackle?

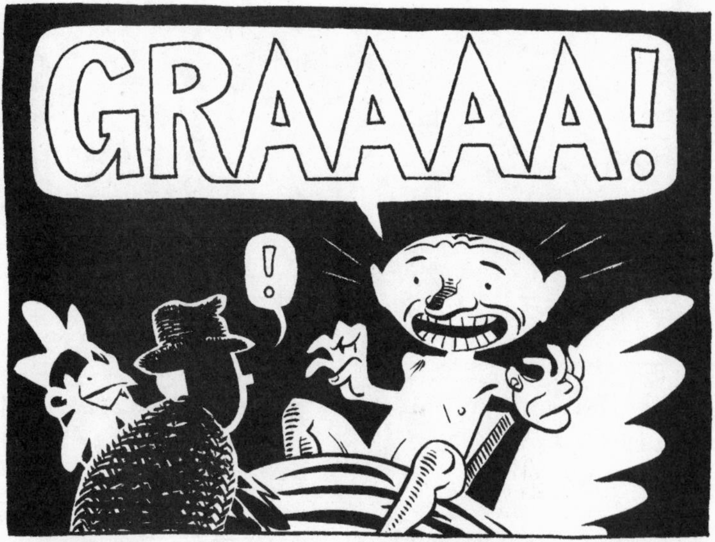
GRAAAA!
!

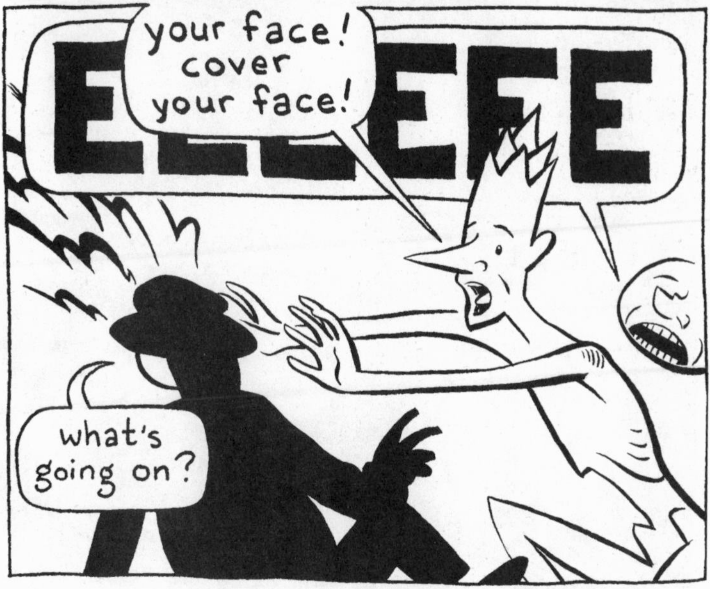
EEEEEE
your face! cover your face!
what's going on?

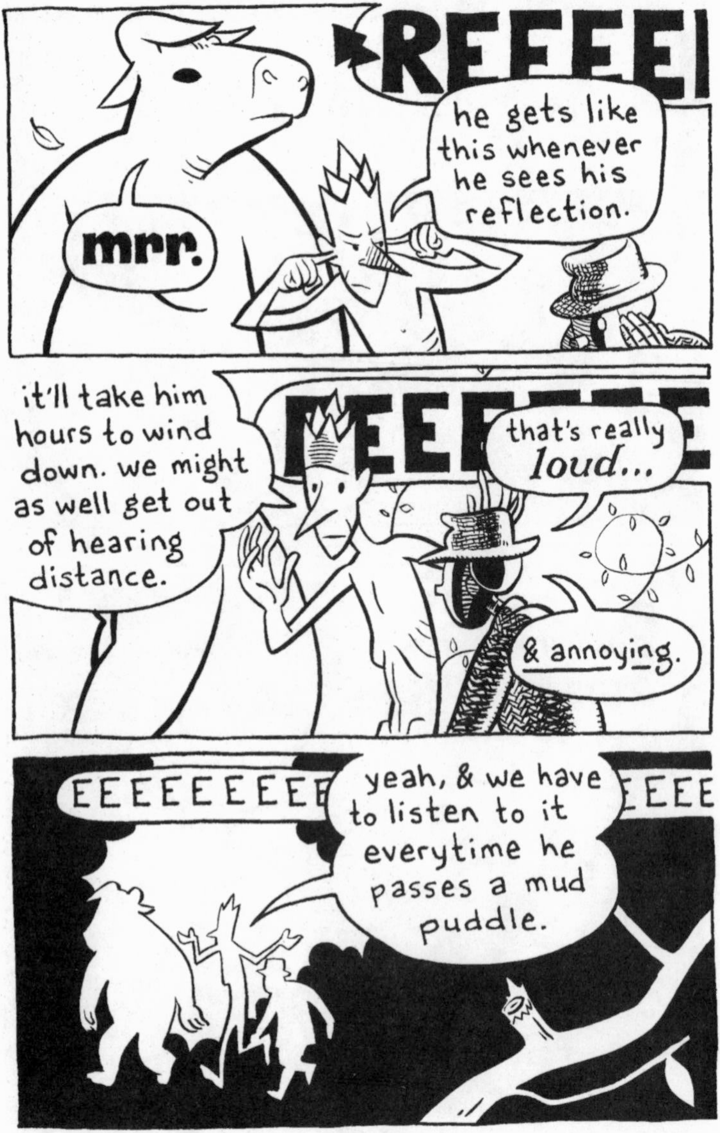
REEEE
mrr.
he gets like this whenever he sees his reflection.
EEEEE
it'll take him hours to wind down. we might as well get out of hearing distance.
that's really *loud*...
& annoying.
EEEEEEEEEEEEE
yeah, & we have to listen to it everytime he passes a mud puddle.

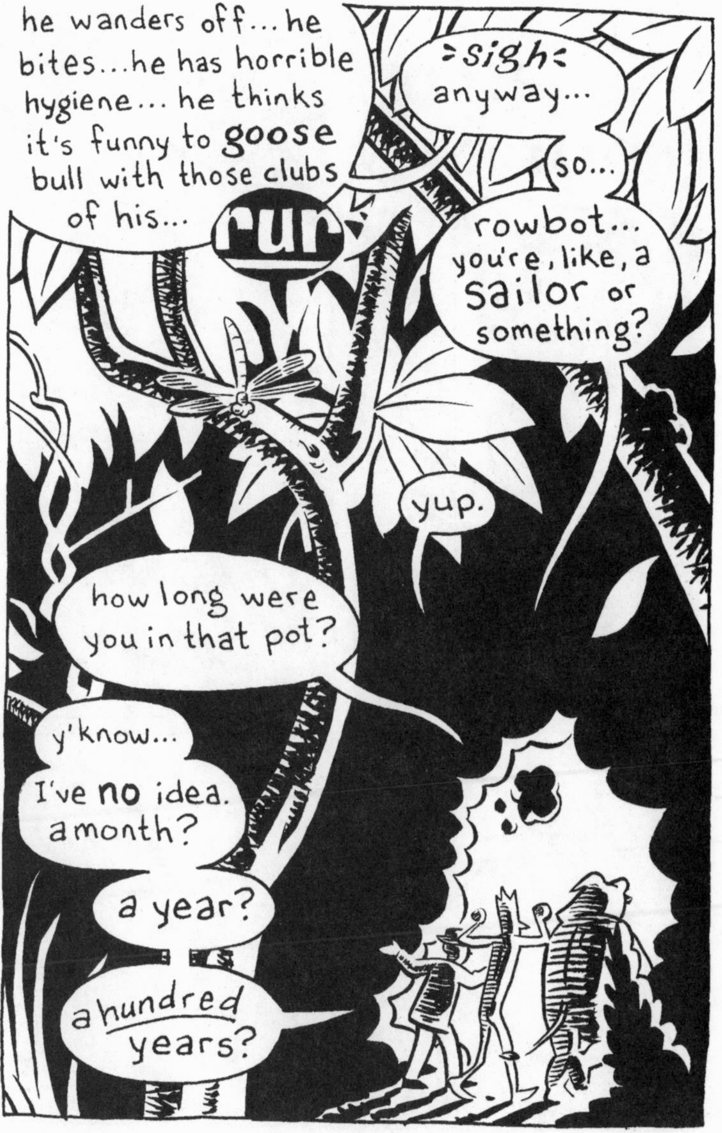

he wanders off... he bites...he has horrible hygiene... he thinks it's funny to goose bull with those clubs of his...
rur
:sigh: anyway...
so...
rowbot... you're, like, a sailor or something?
yup.
how long were you in that pot?
y'know...
I've no idea. a month?
a year?
a hundred years?

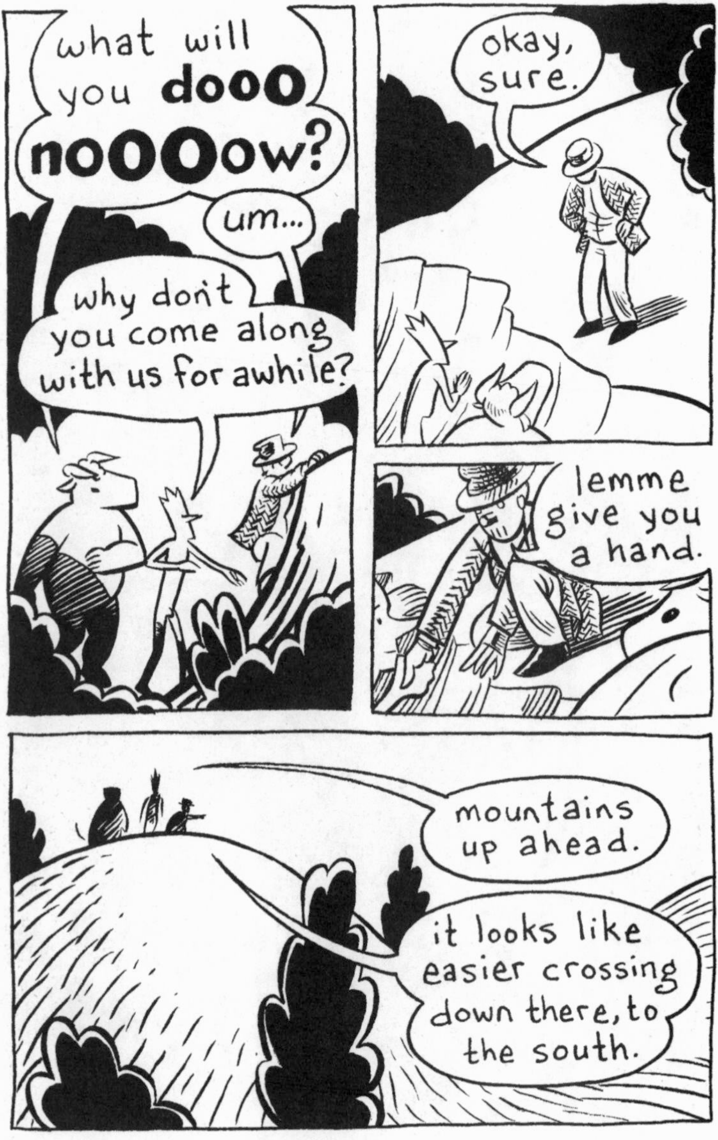
what will you doooO nooOOow?
um...
why don't you come along with us for awhile?
okay, sure.
lemme give you a hand.
mountains up ahead.
it looks like easier crossing down there, to the south.

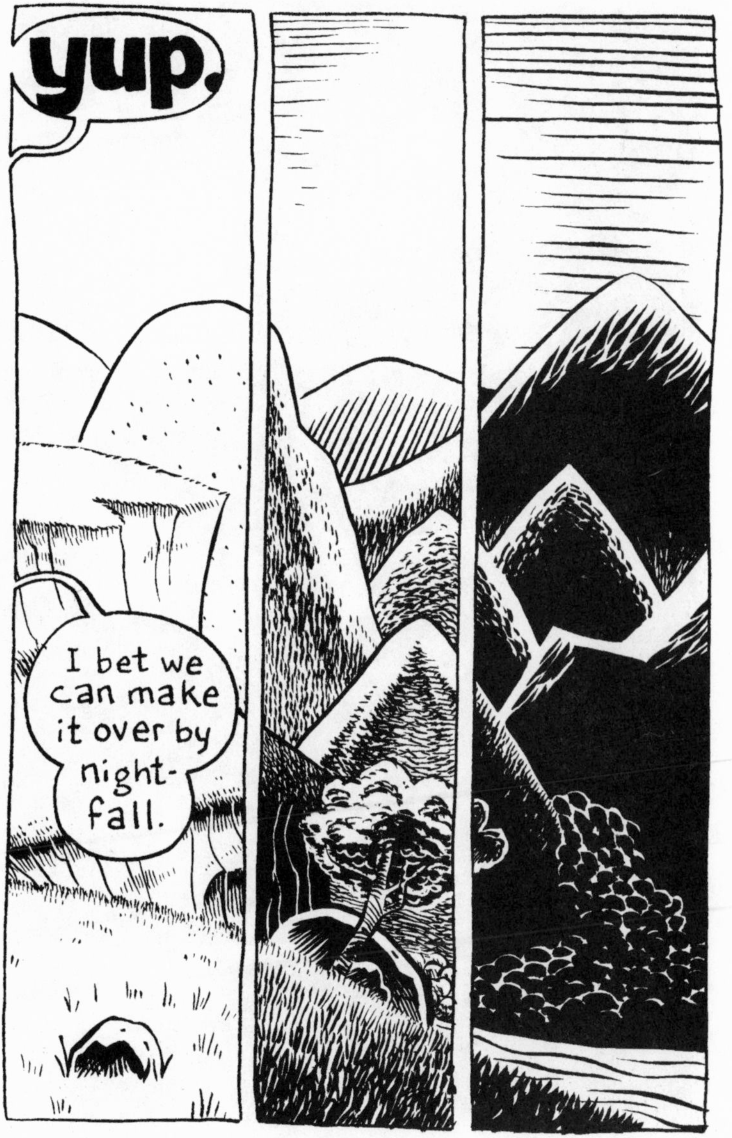
yup.
I bet we can make it over by night-fall.

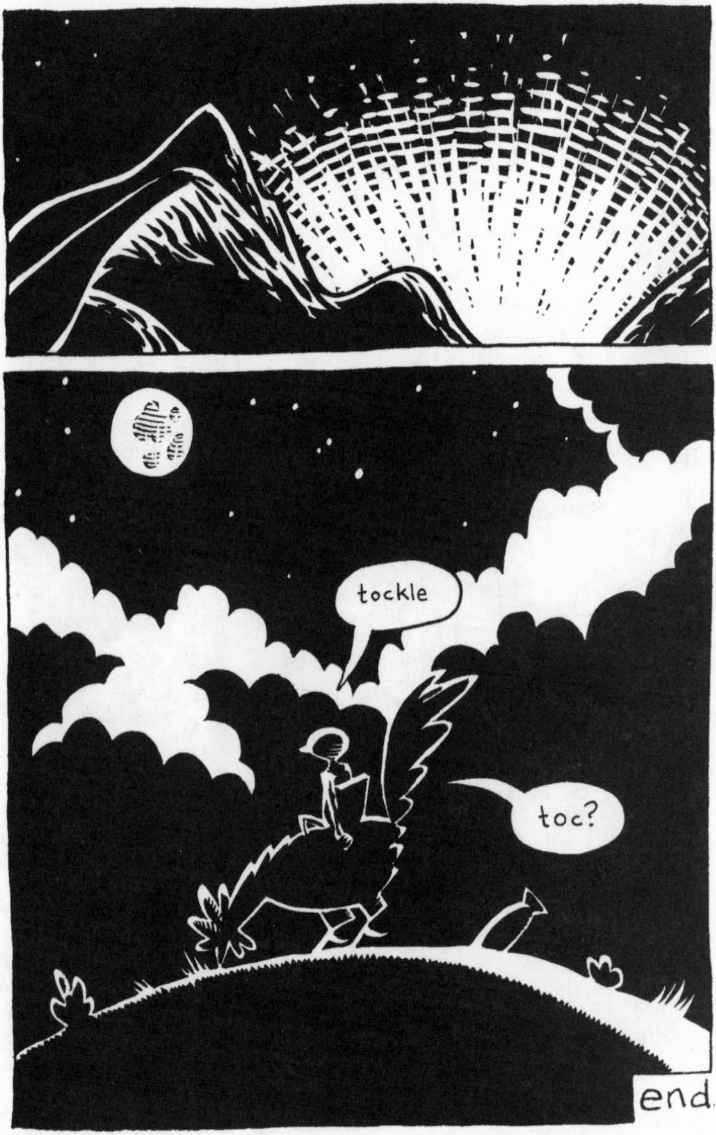
tockle
toc?
end.

rowbot, bull,& delaware thistle

in

frozen

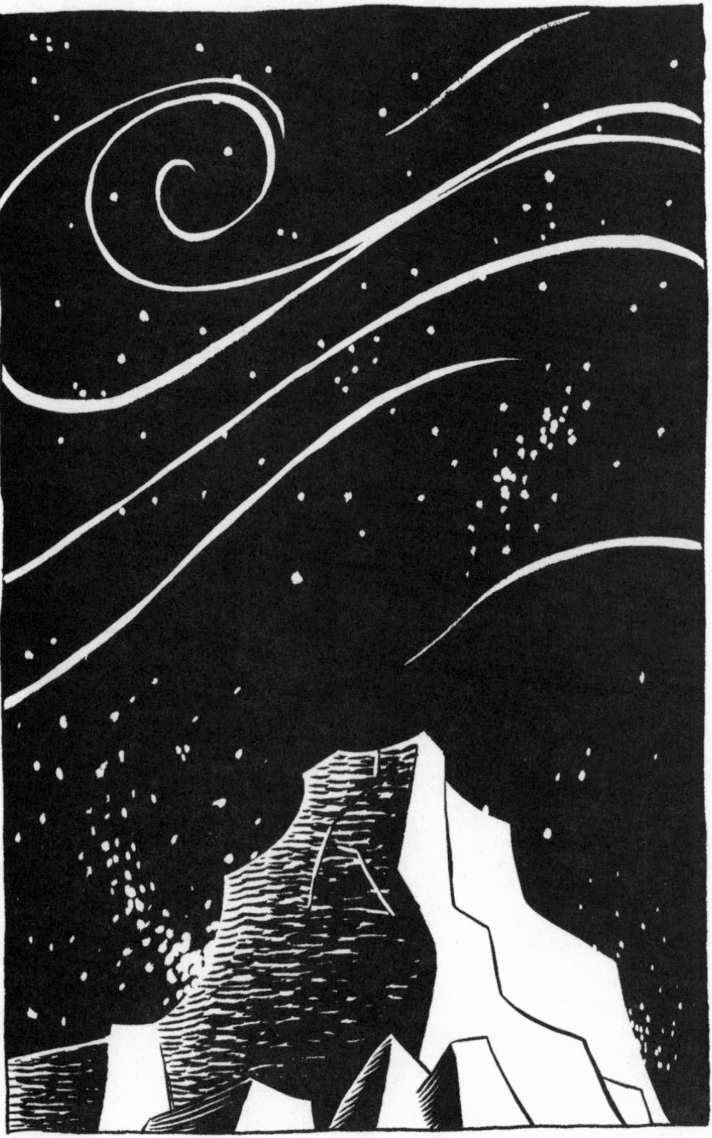

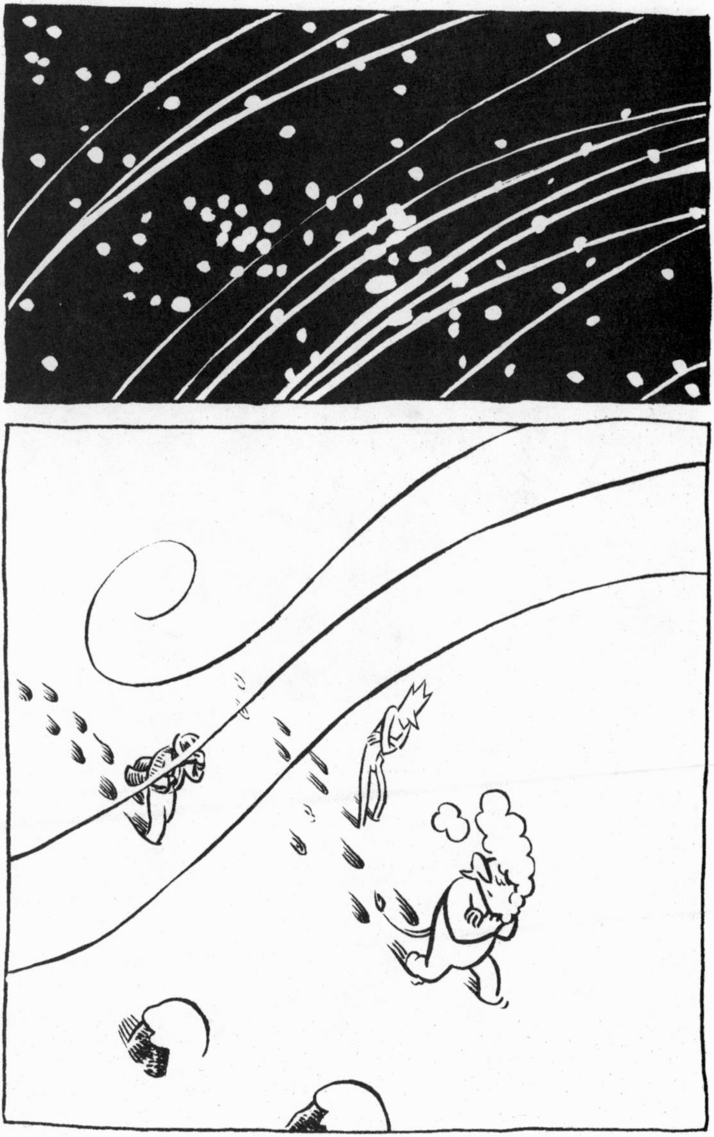

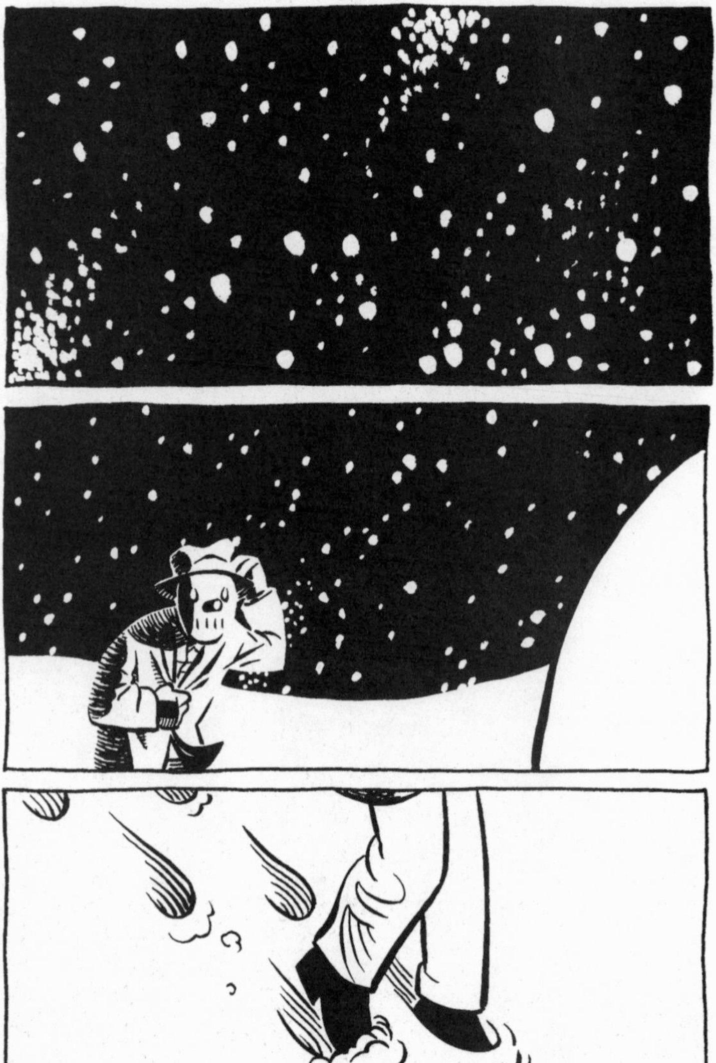

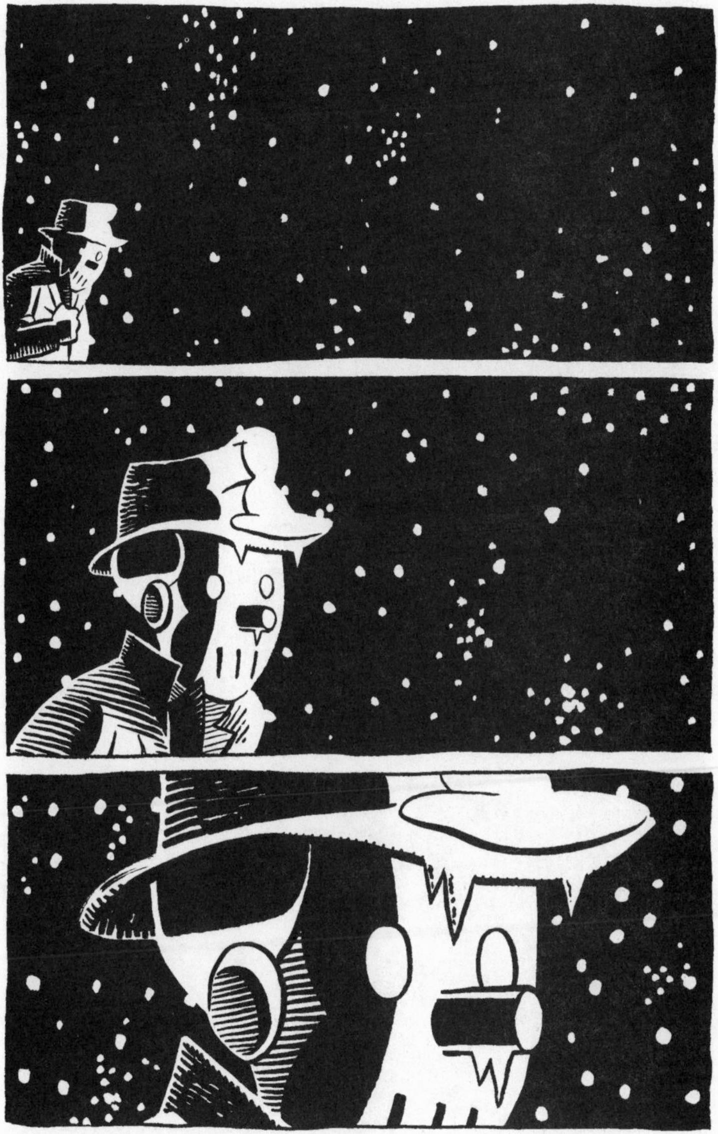

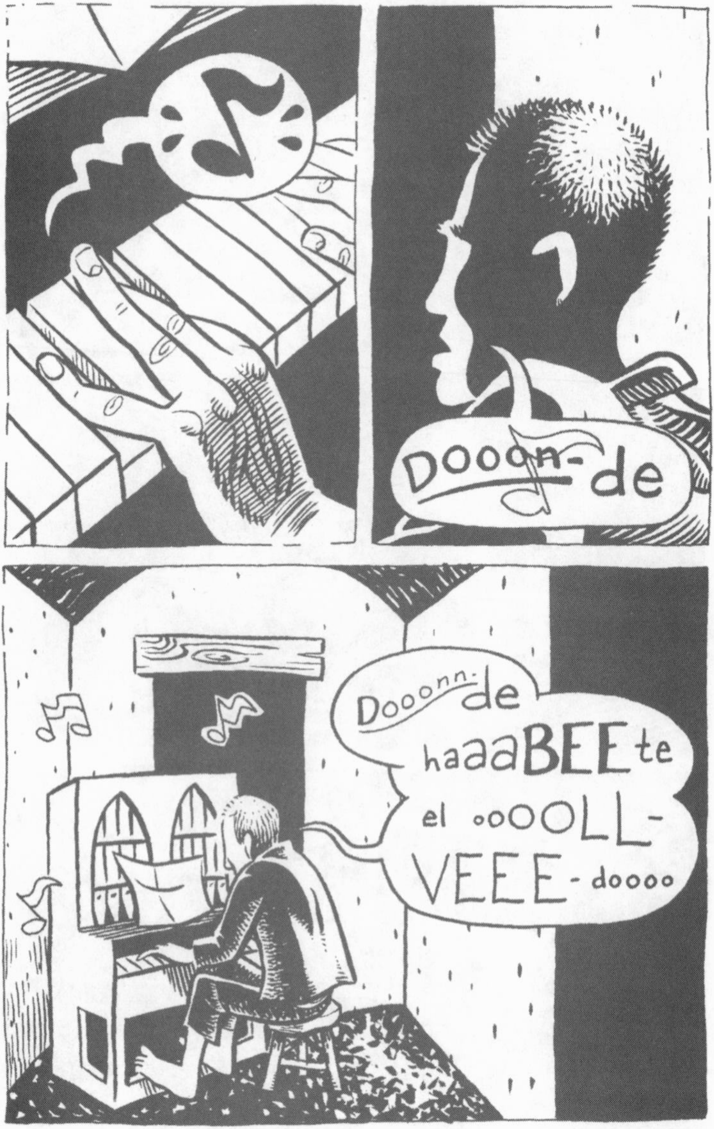
Dooon-de
Dooonn-de haaaBEEte el ooOOLL-VEEE-doooo

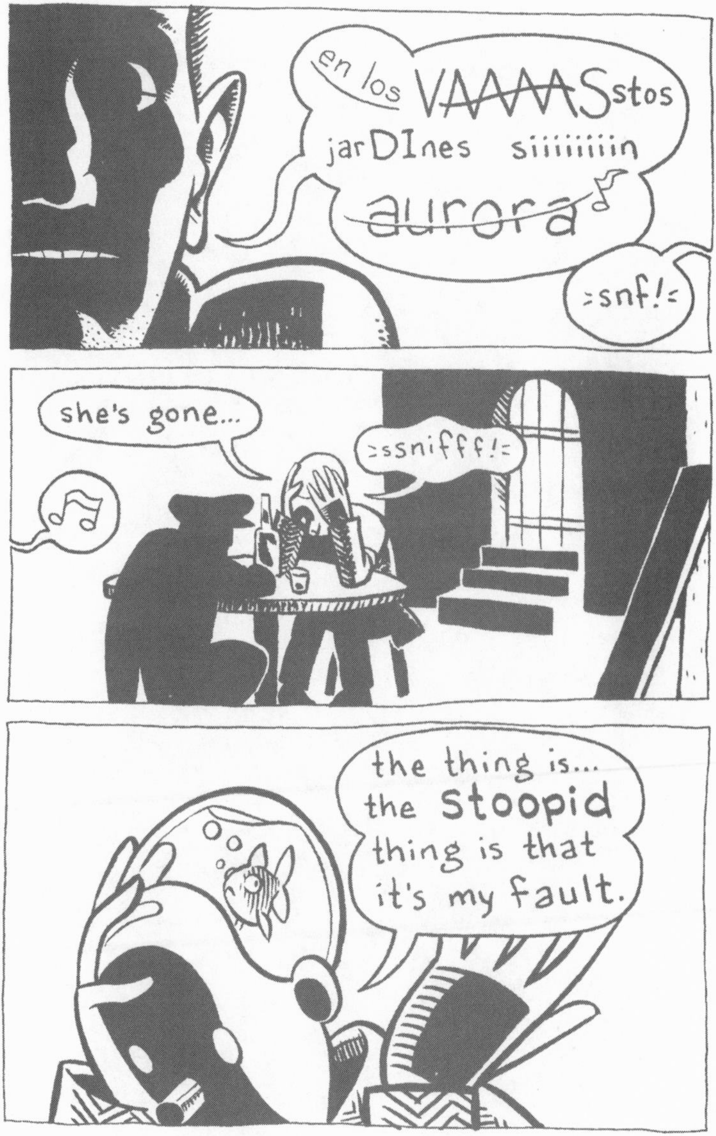
en los VAAAASstos
jarDInes siiiiiiiiin
aurora
=snf!=
she's gone...
=ssnifff!=
the thing is...
the Stoopid
thing is that
it's my fault.

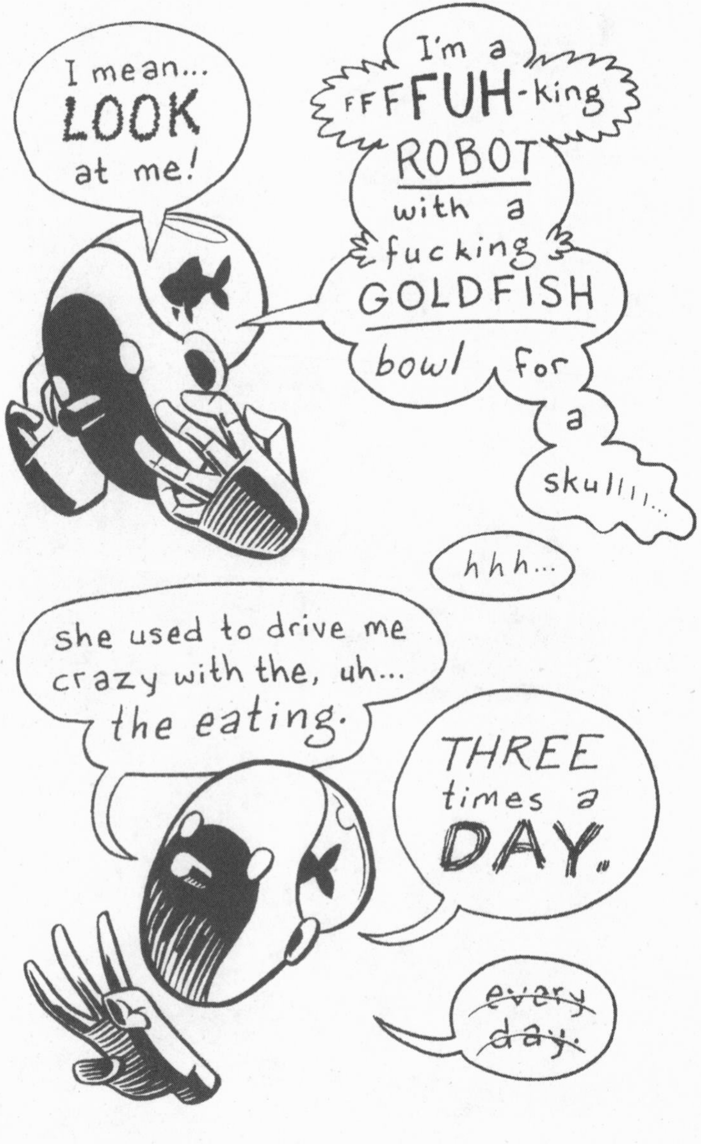
I mean... LOOK at me!
I'm a fffFUH-king ROBOT with a fucking GOLDFISH bowl for a skulllll...
hhh...
she used to drive me crazy with the, uh... the eating.
THREE times a DAY."
every day.

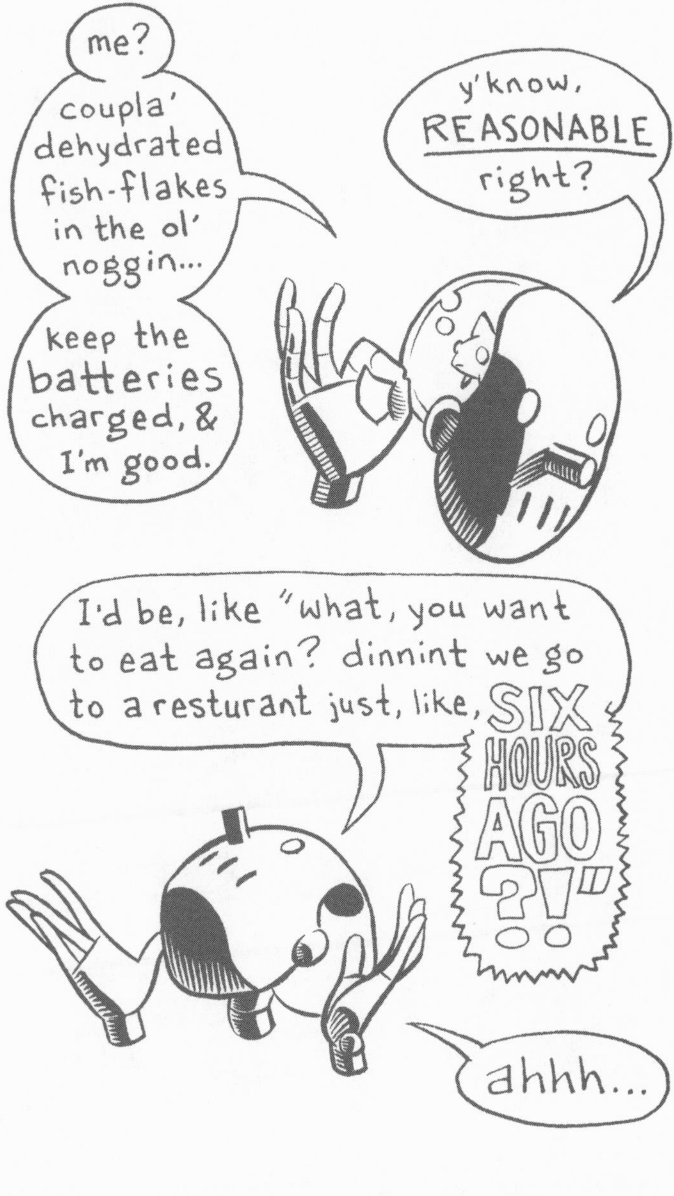
me?
coupla' dehydrated fish-flakes in the ol' noggin...
keep the batteries charged, & I'm good.
y'know, REASONABLE right?
I'd be, like "what, you want to eat again? dinnint we go to a resturant just, like, SIX HOURS AGO ?!"
ahhh...

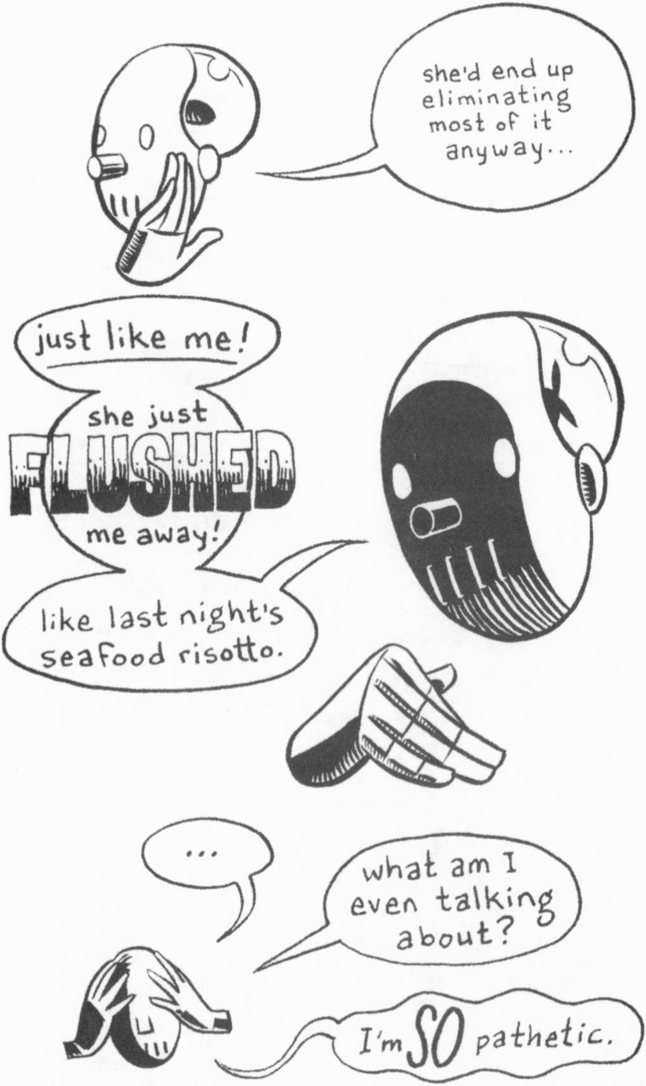
she'd end up eliminating most of it anyway...
just like me!
she just FLUSHED me away!
like last night's seafood risotto.
...
what am I even talking about?
I'm SO pathetic.

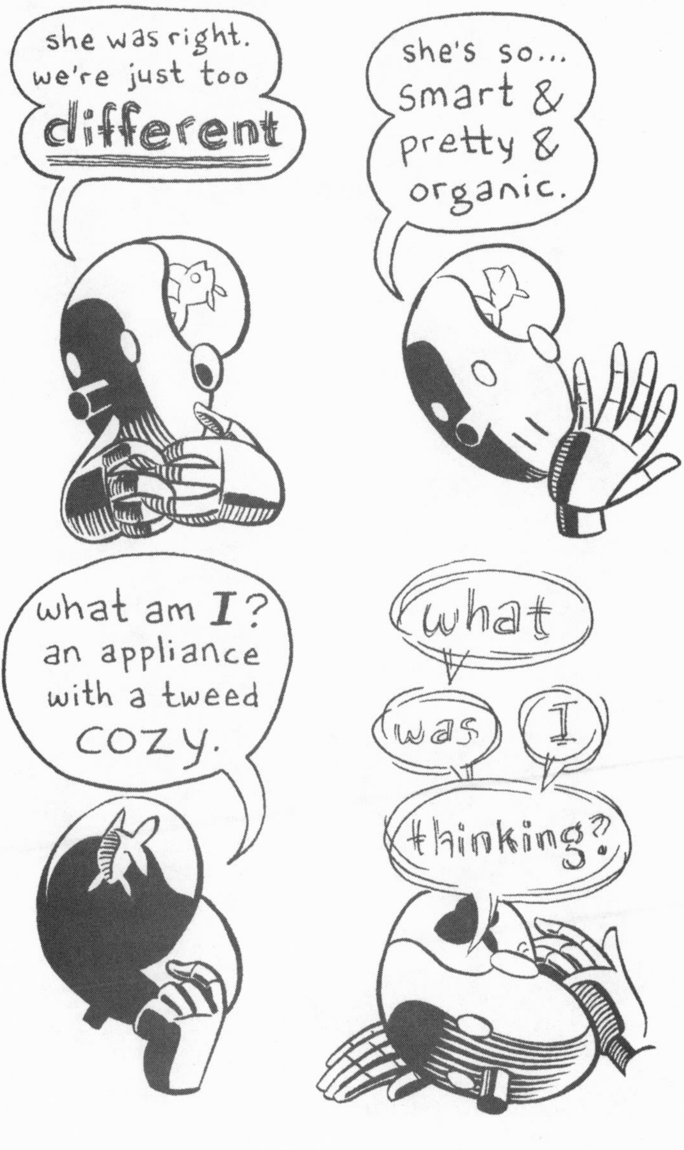
she was right. we're just too different
she's so... smart & pretty & organic.
what am I? an appliance with a tweed cozy.
what
was
I
thinking?

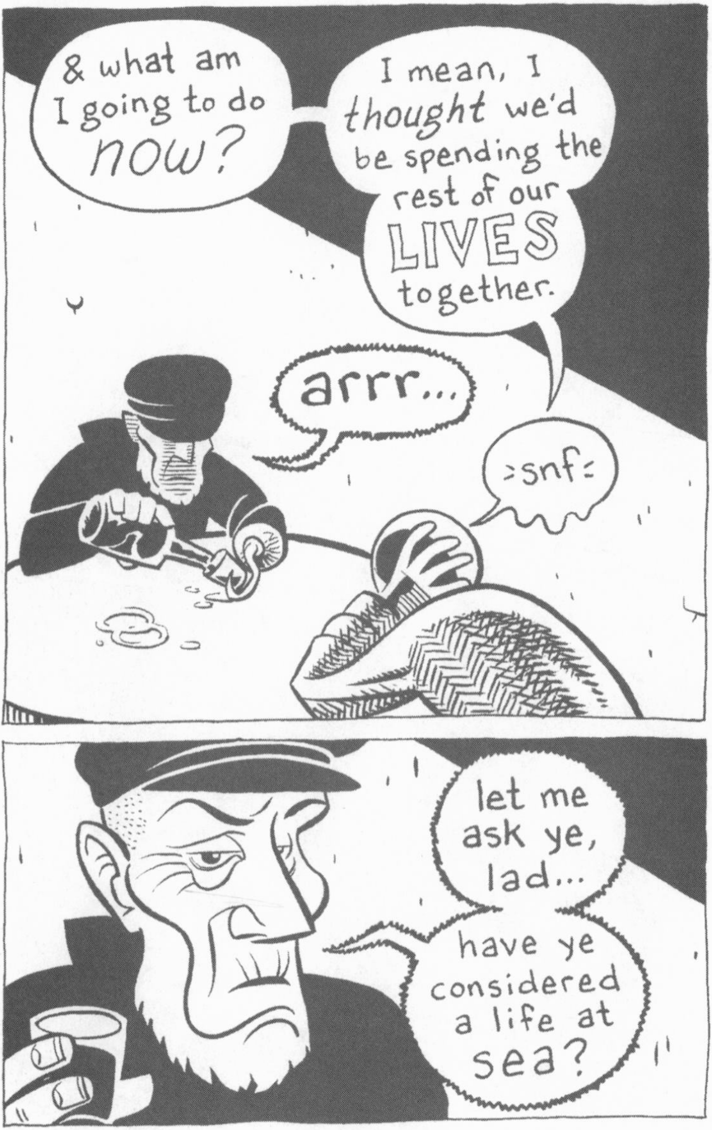
& what am I going to do now?
I mean, I thought we'd be spending the rest of our LIVES together.
arrr...
>snf<
let me ask ye, lad...
have ye considered a life at sea?

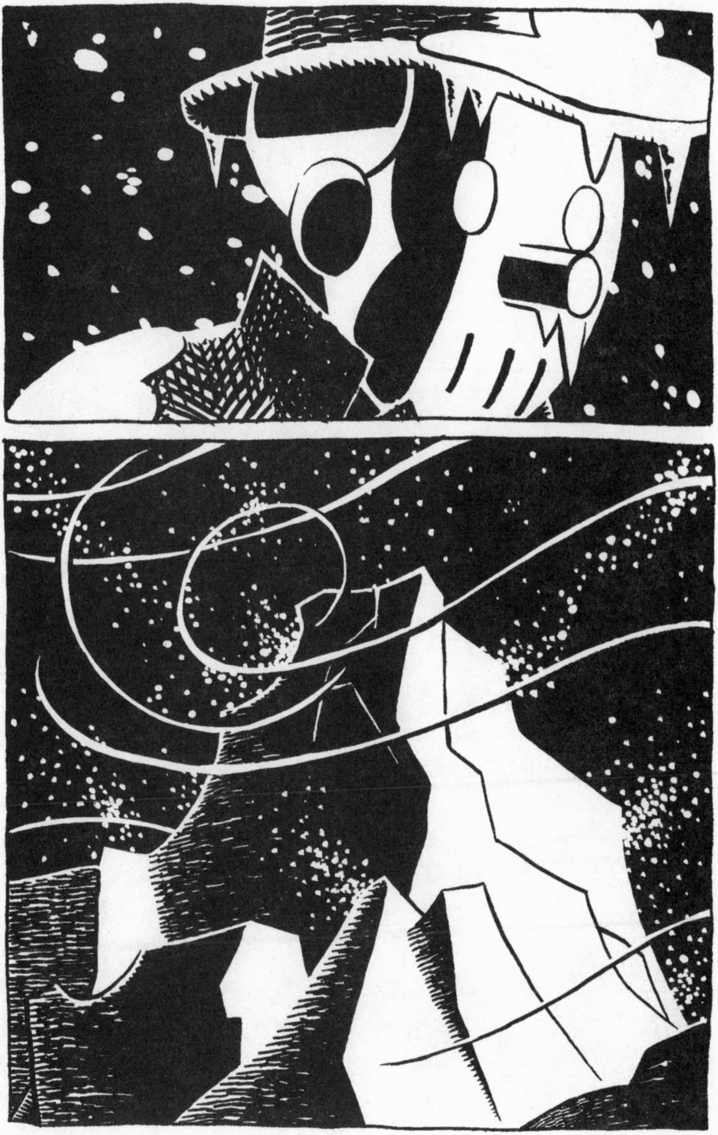

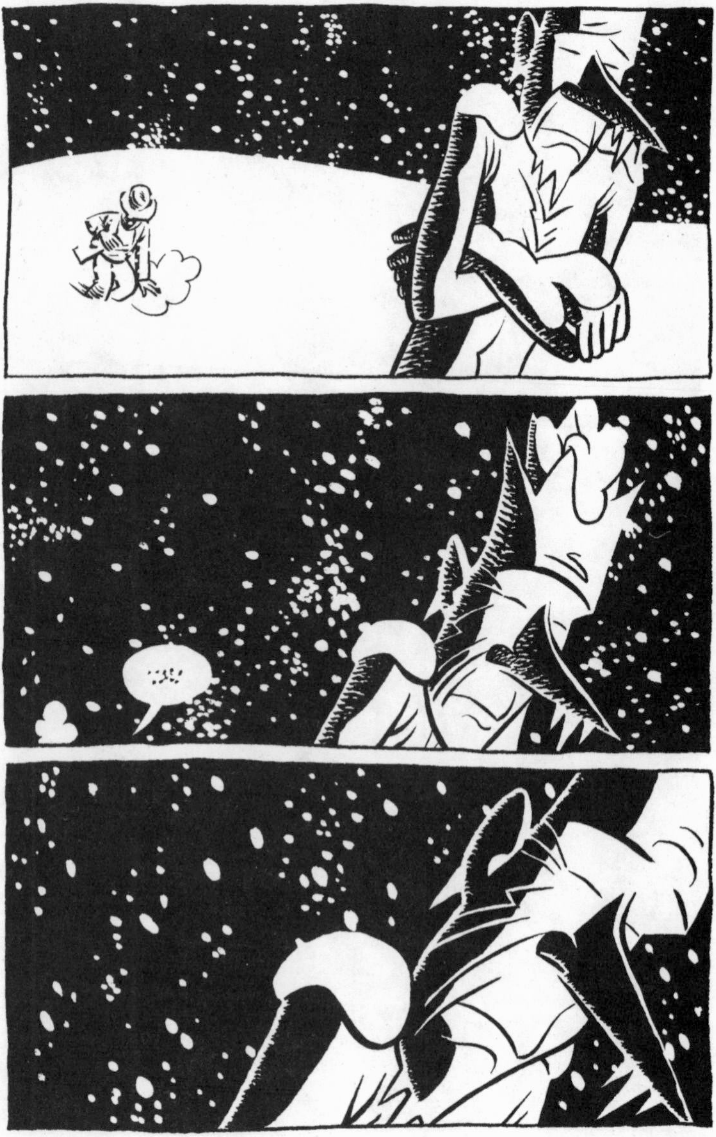

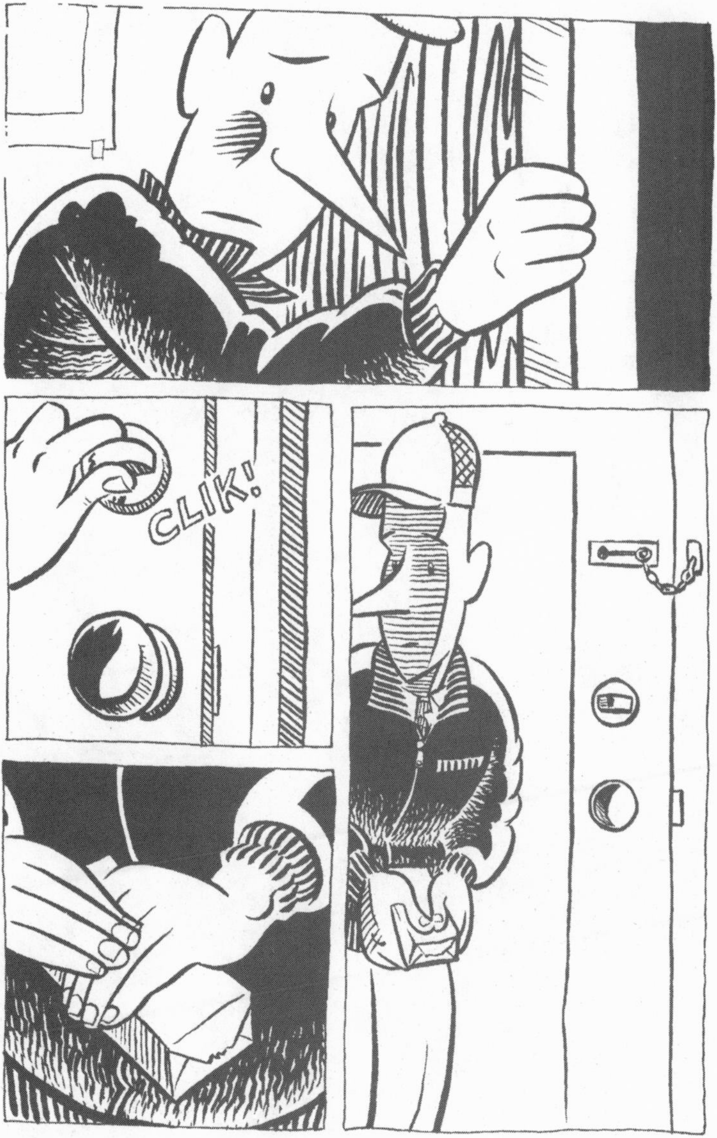
CLIK!

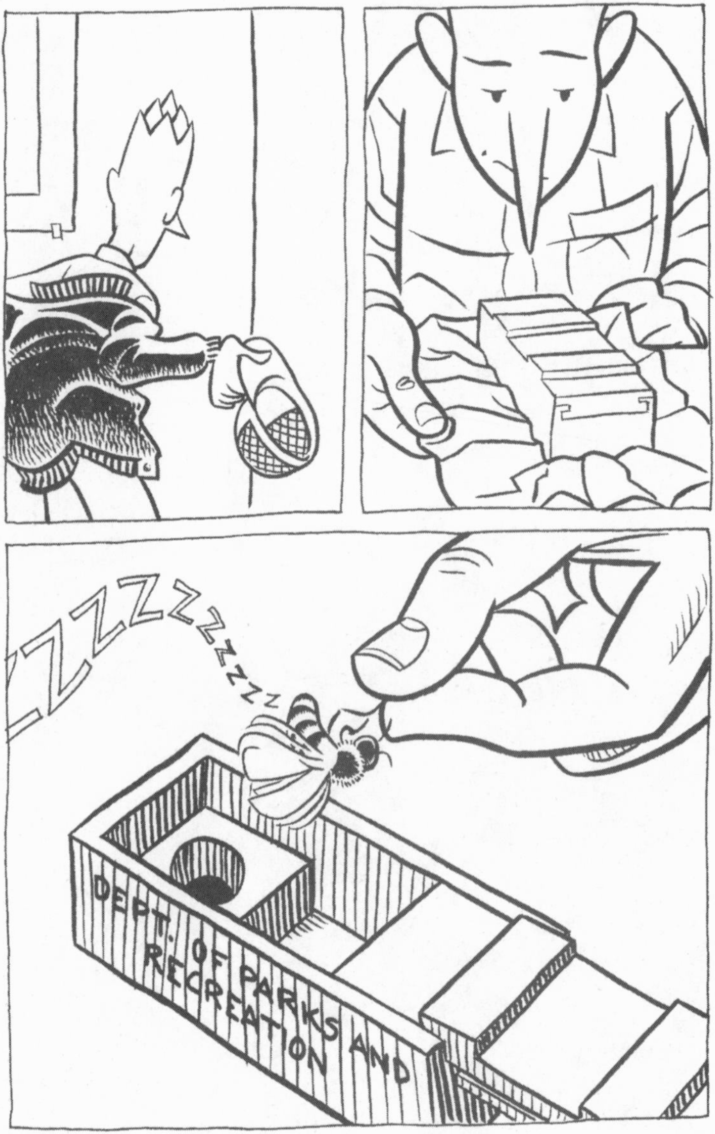
DEPT. OF PARKS AND
RECREATION

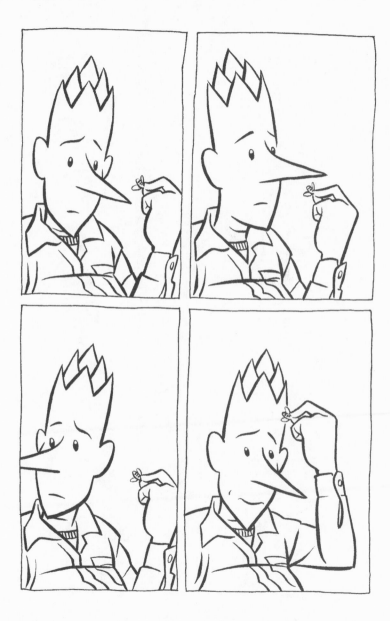

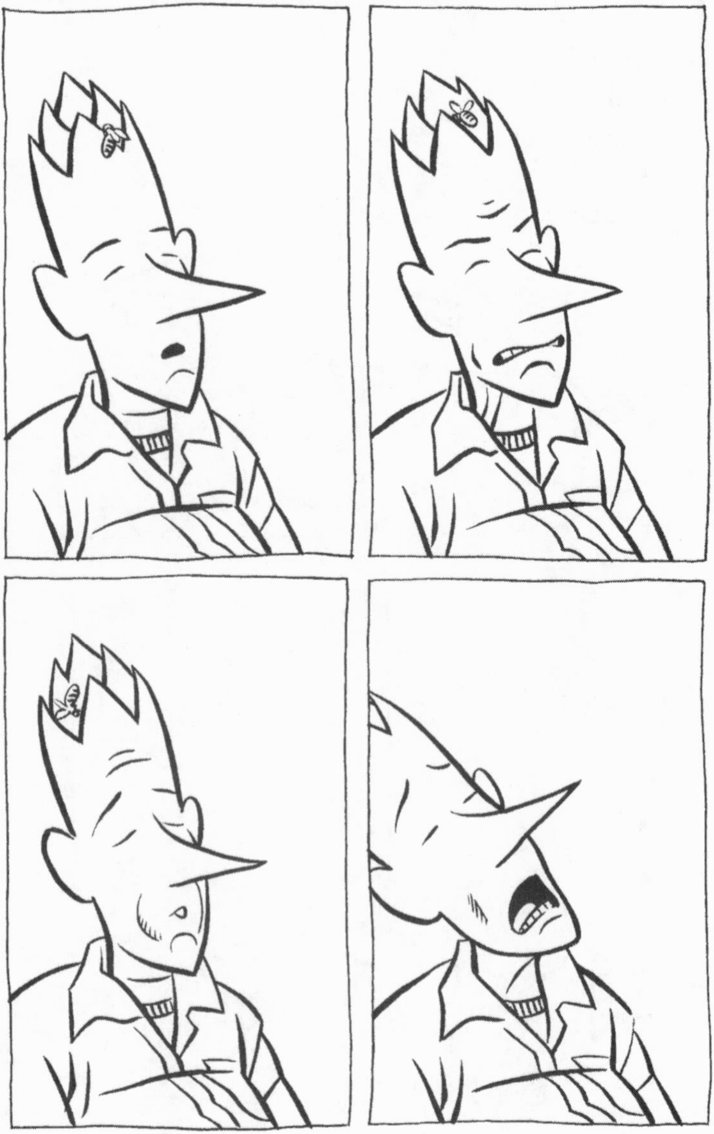

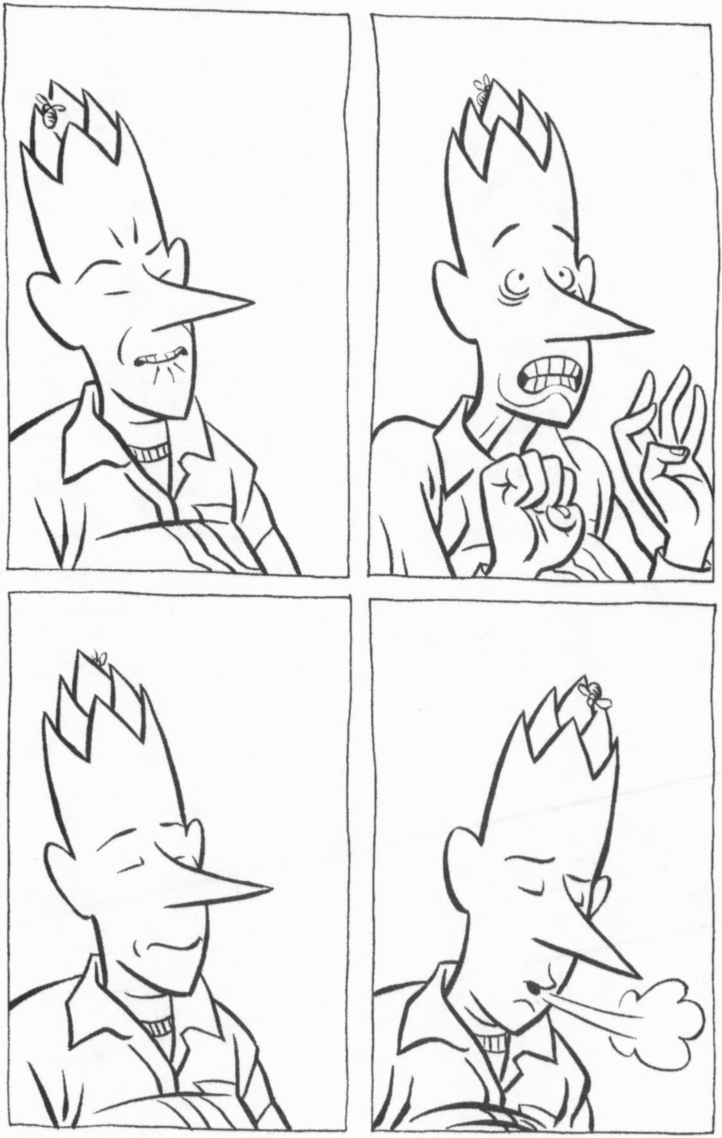

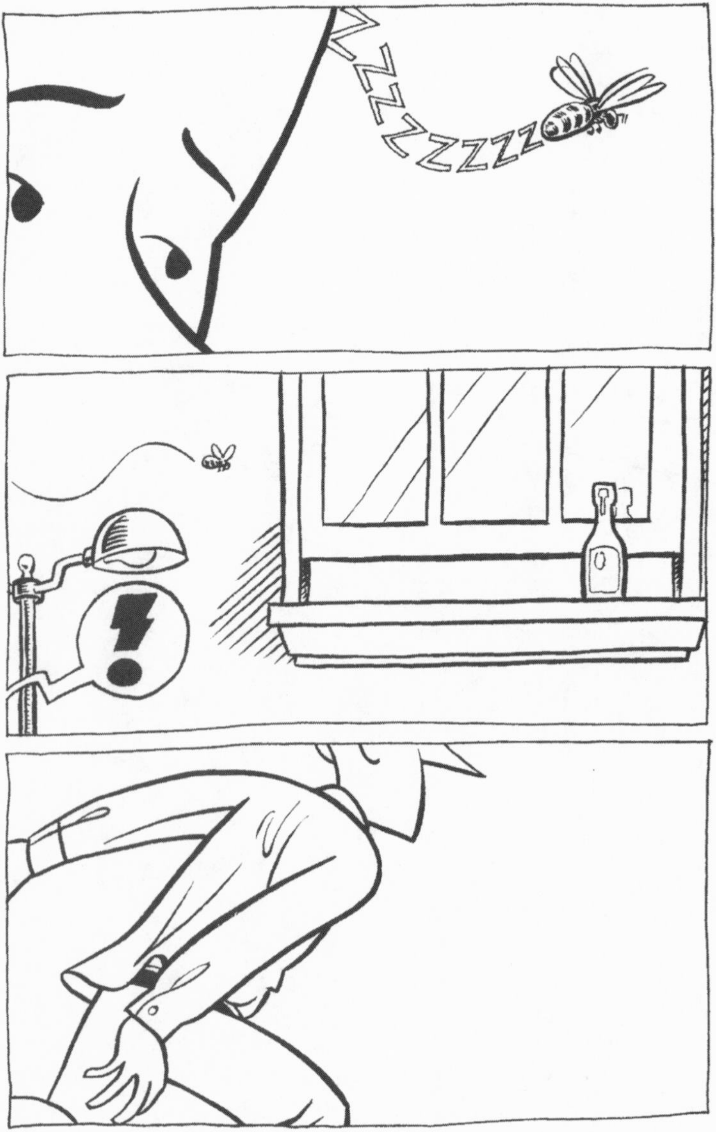
ZZZZZZZZ
!

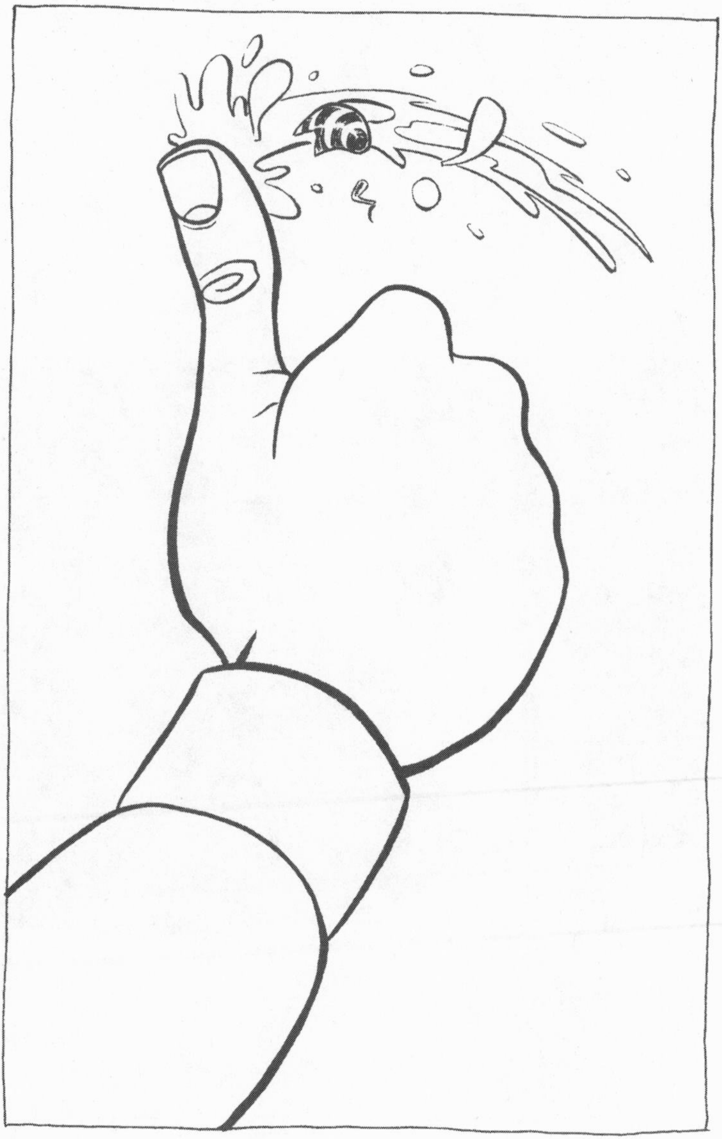

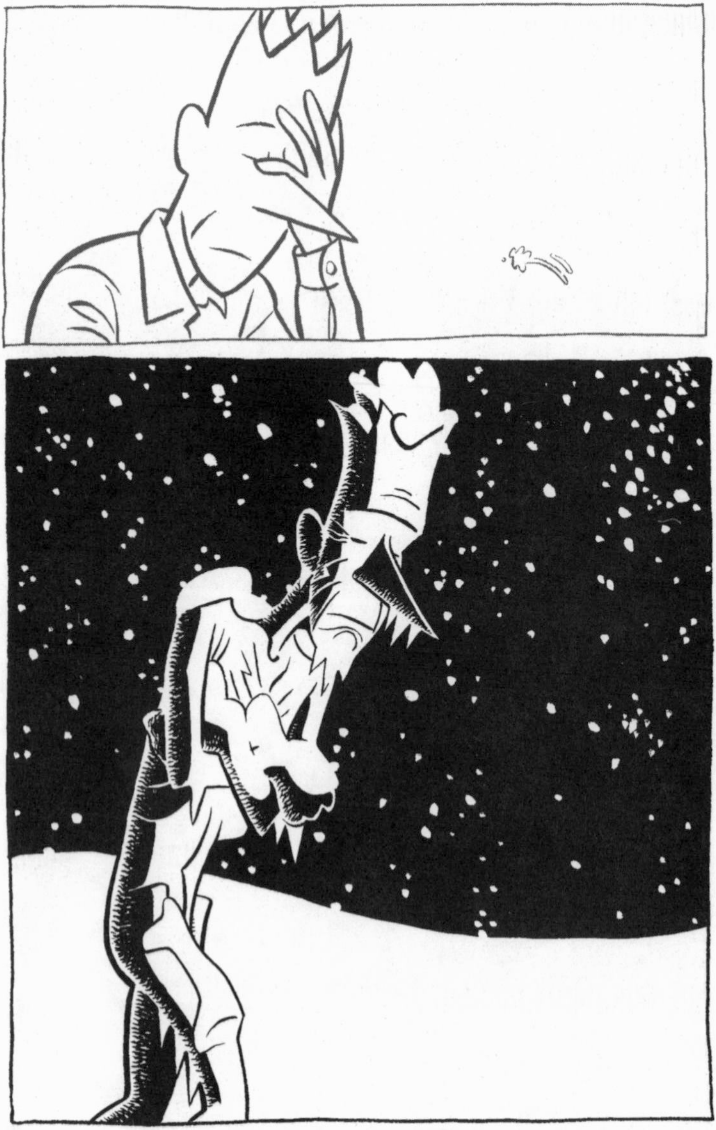

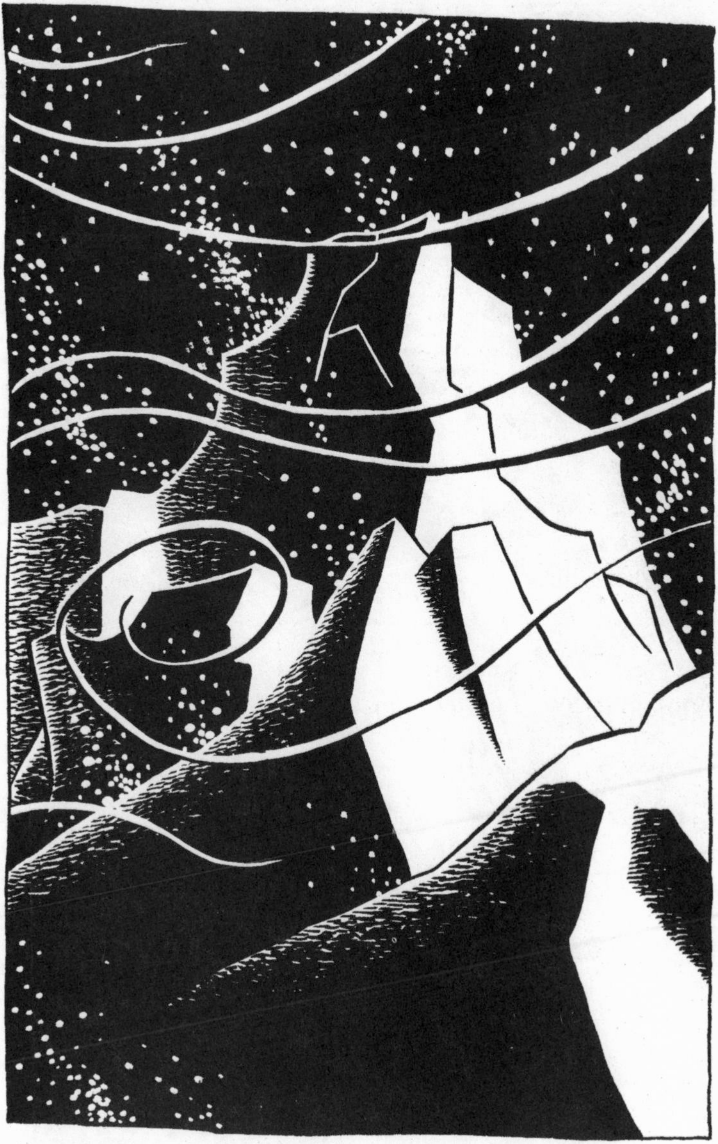

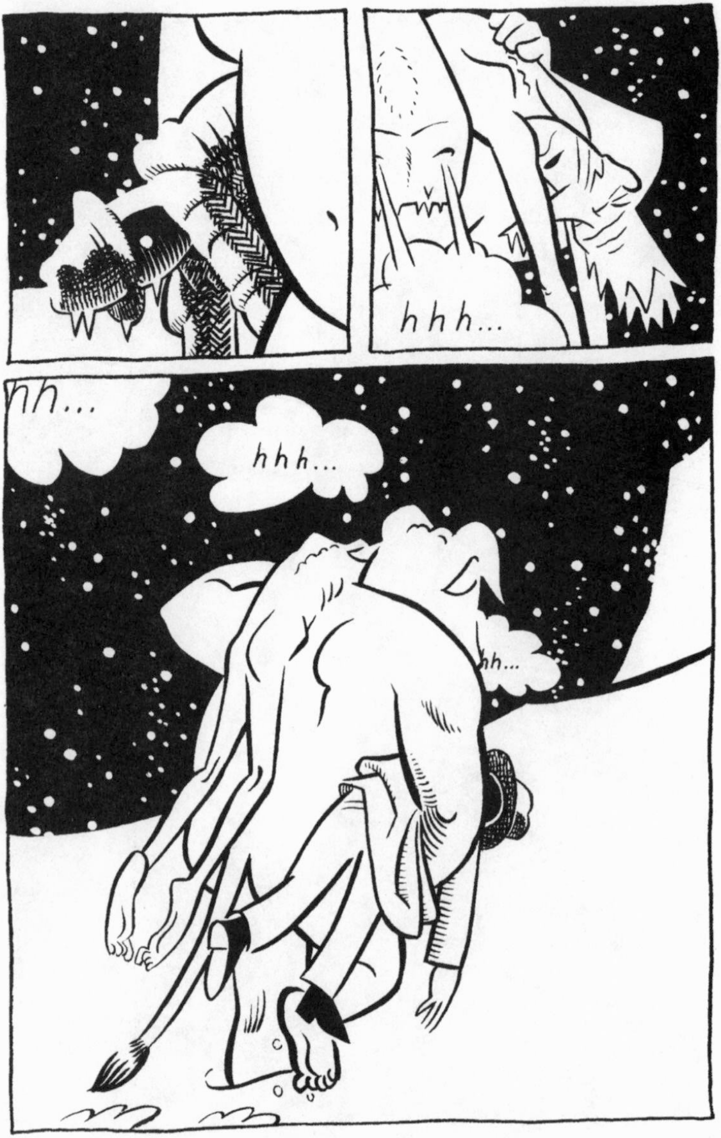
hhh...
hh...
hhh...
hh...

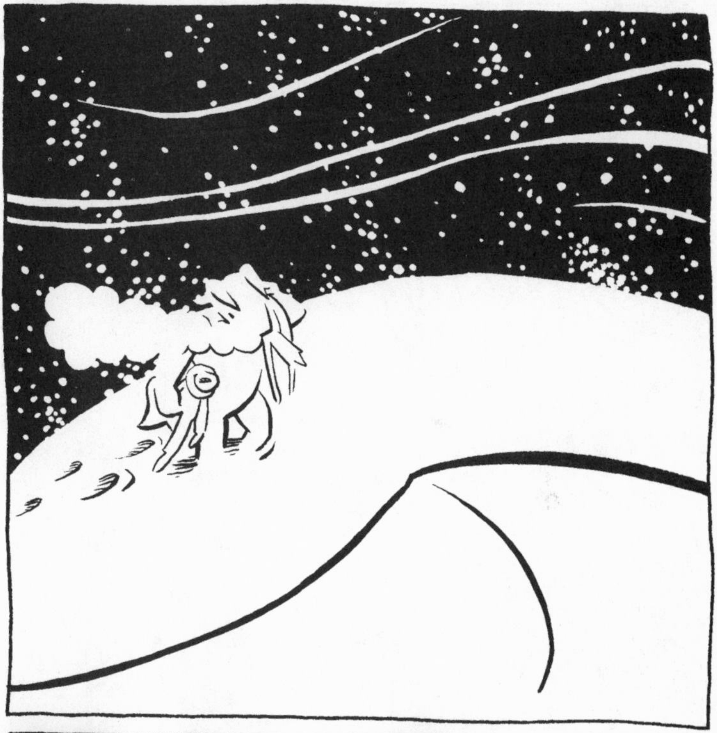
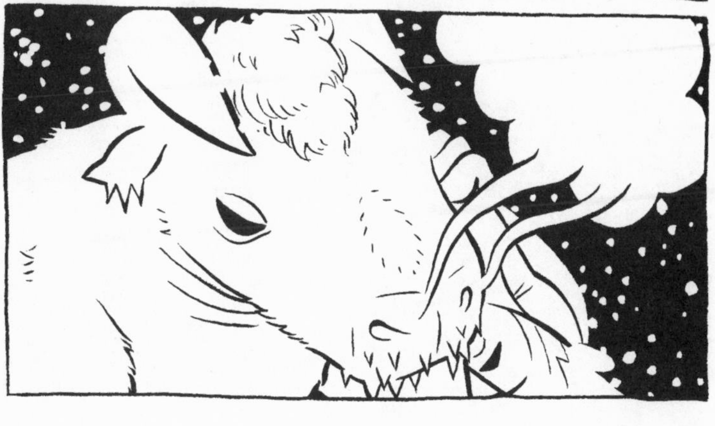

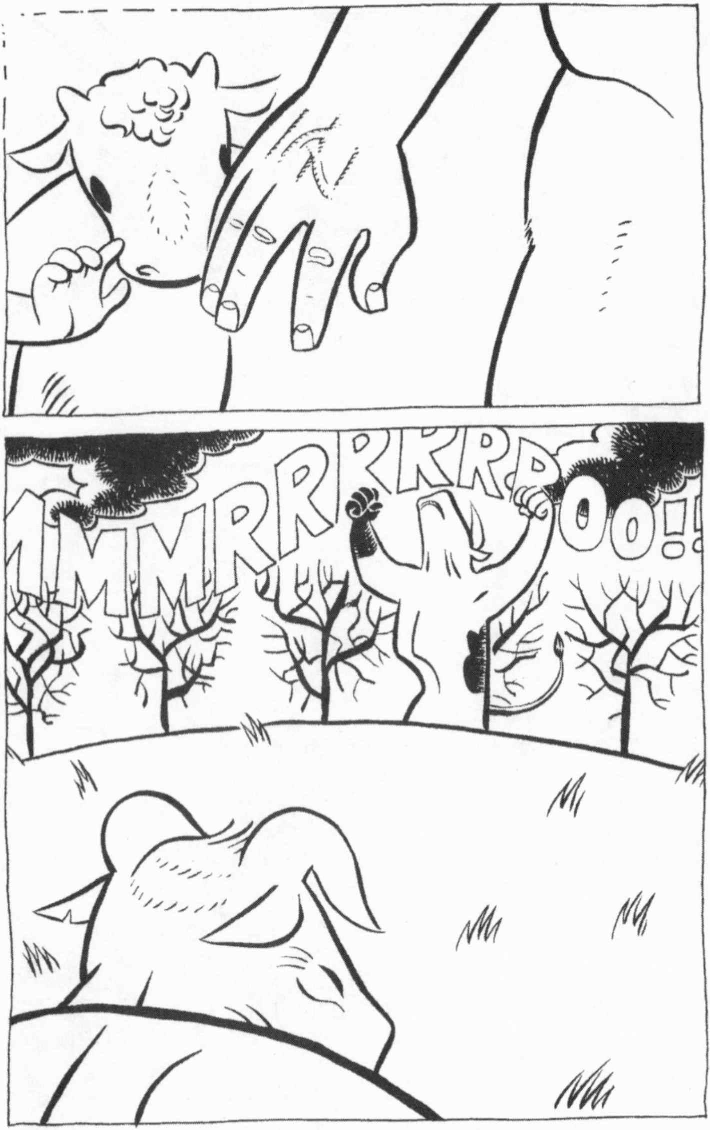
MMMRRRRRROO!!

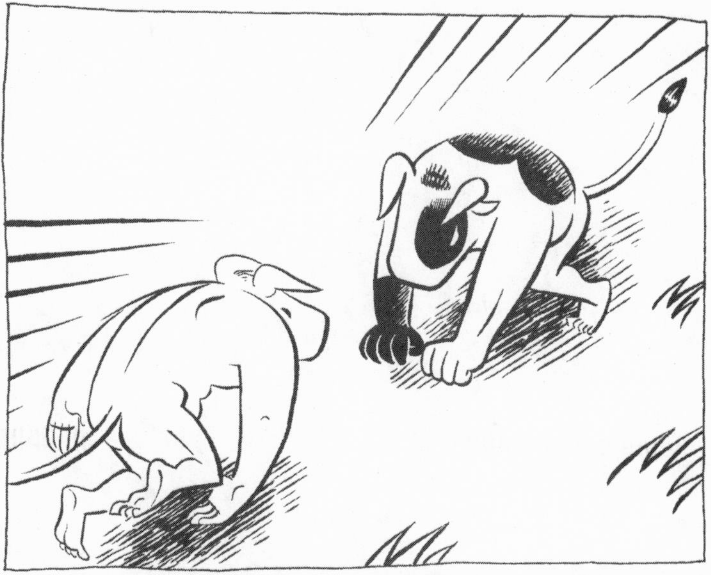

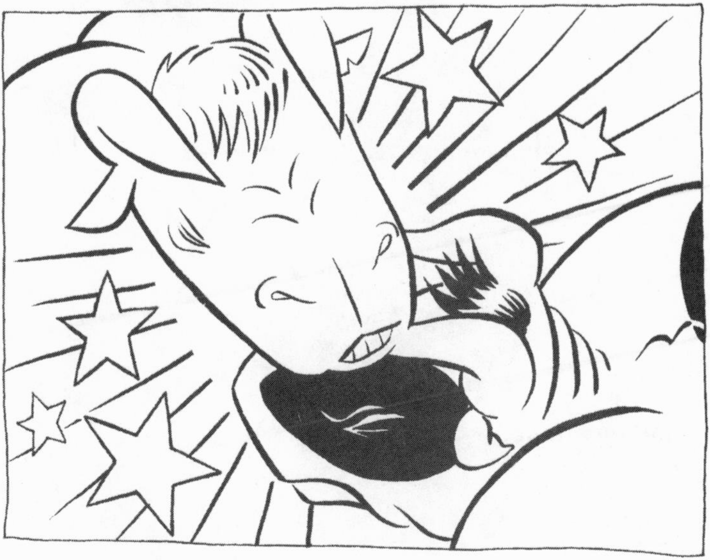

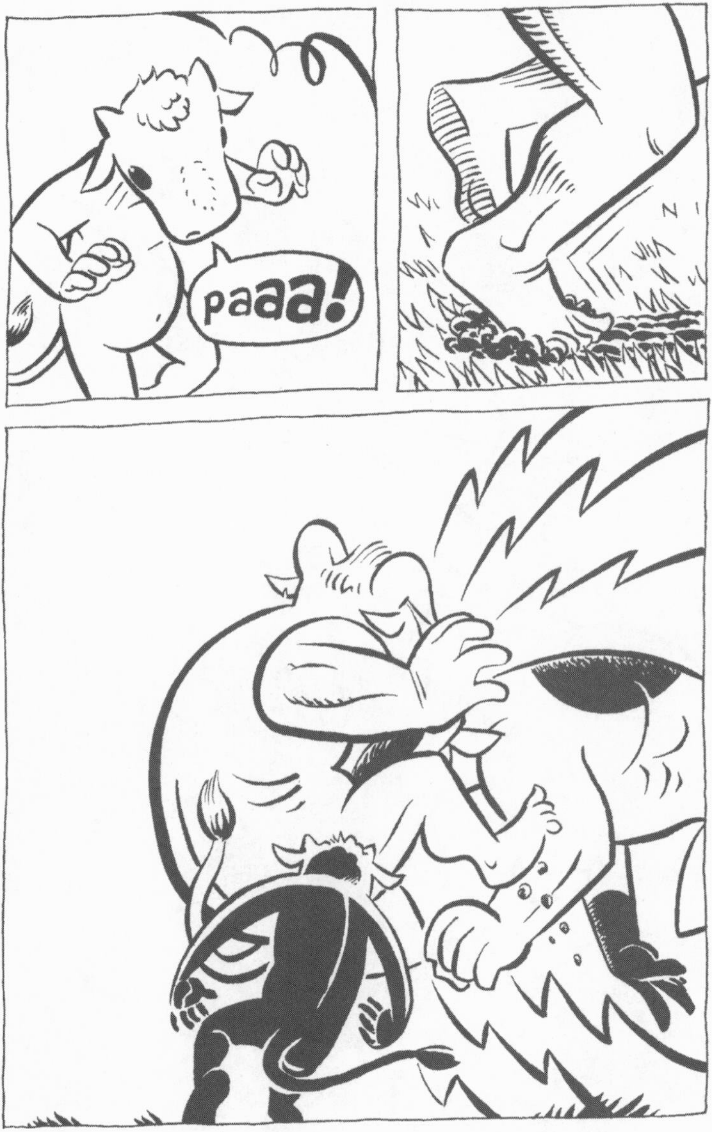
paaa!

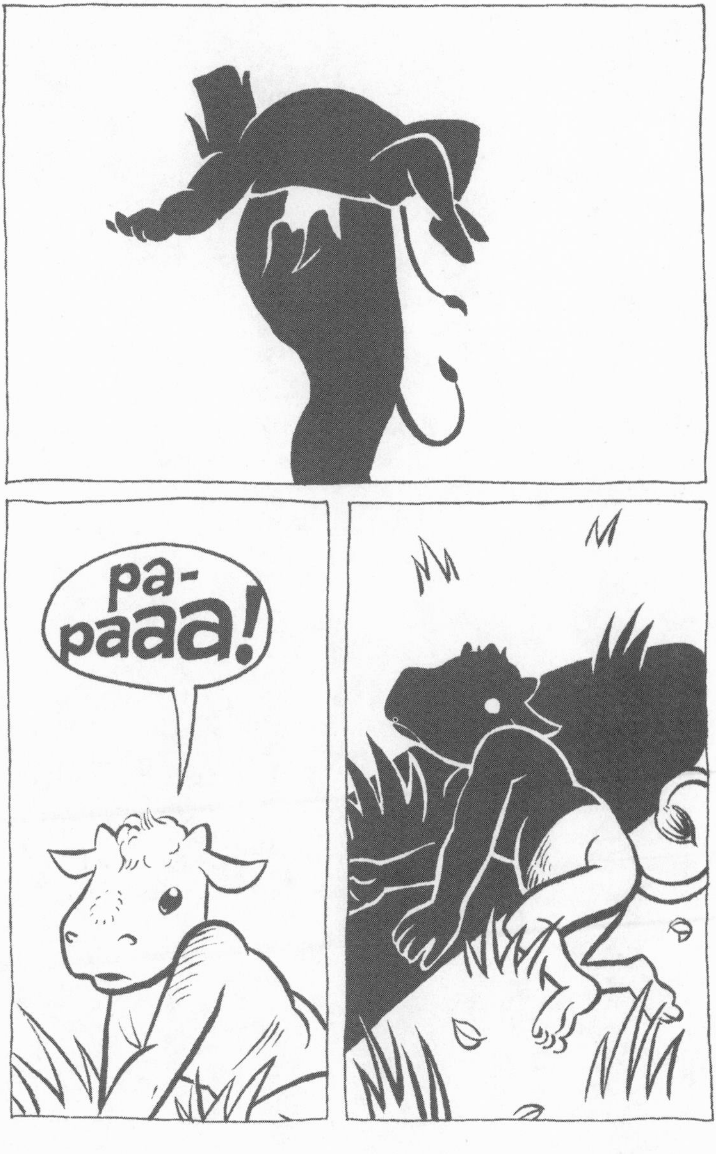
pa-
paaa!

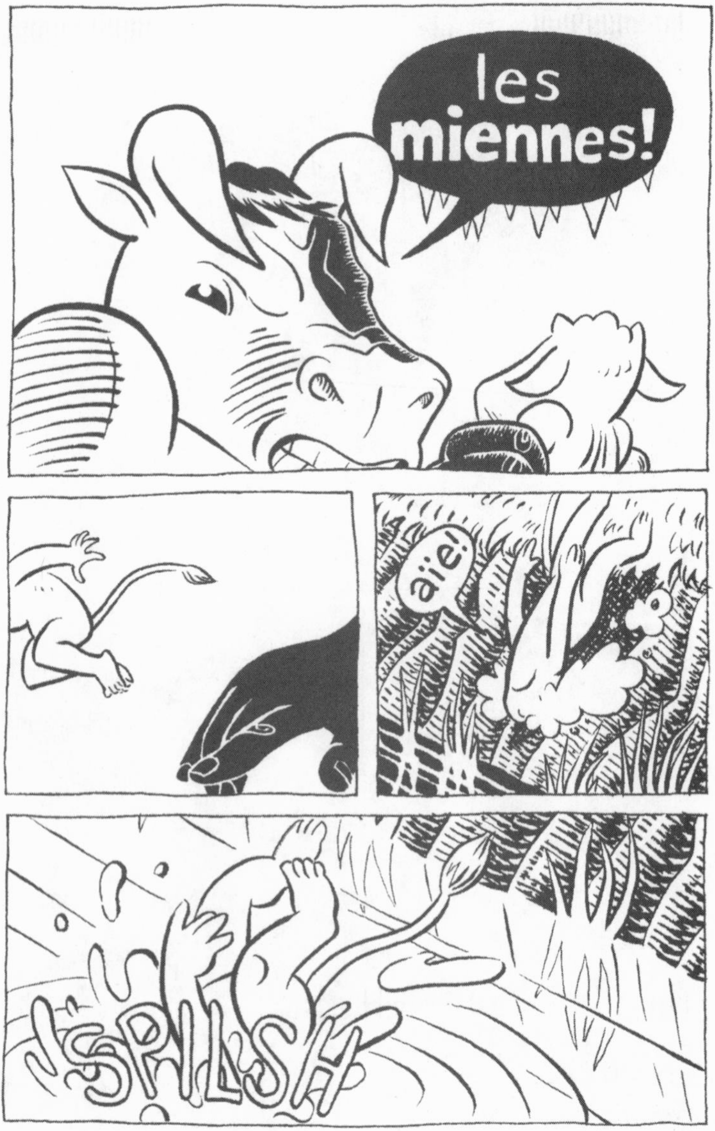
les
miennes!
aïe!
SPILSH

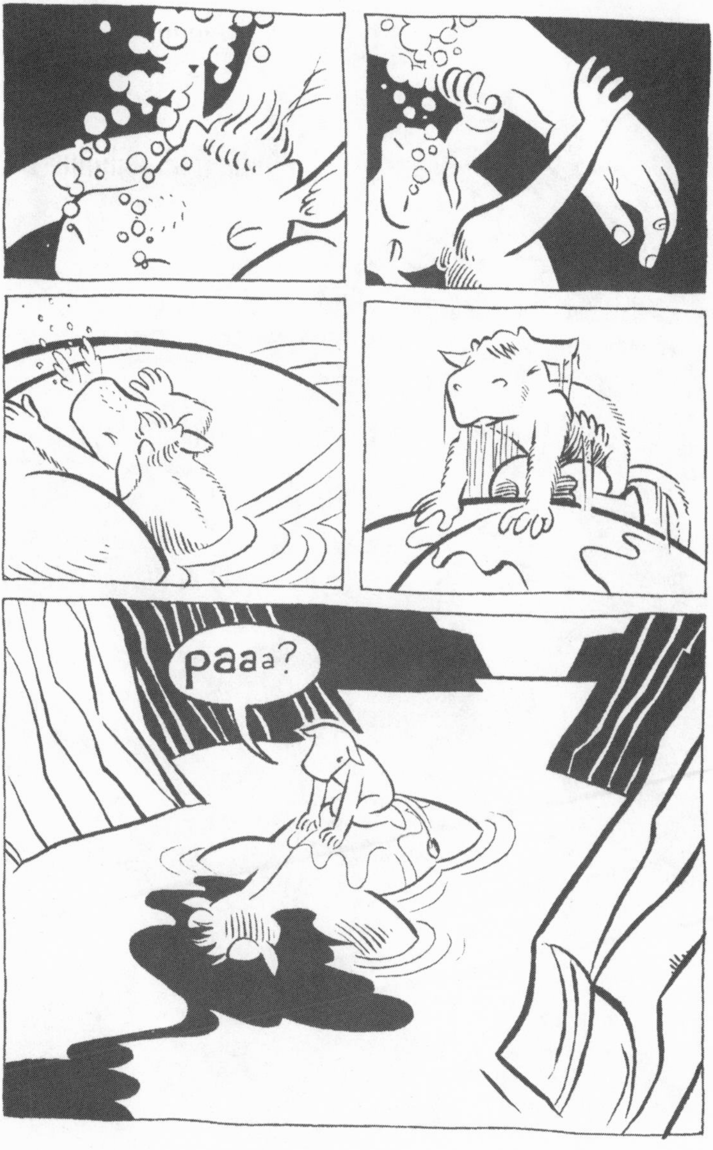
paaa?

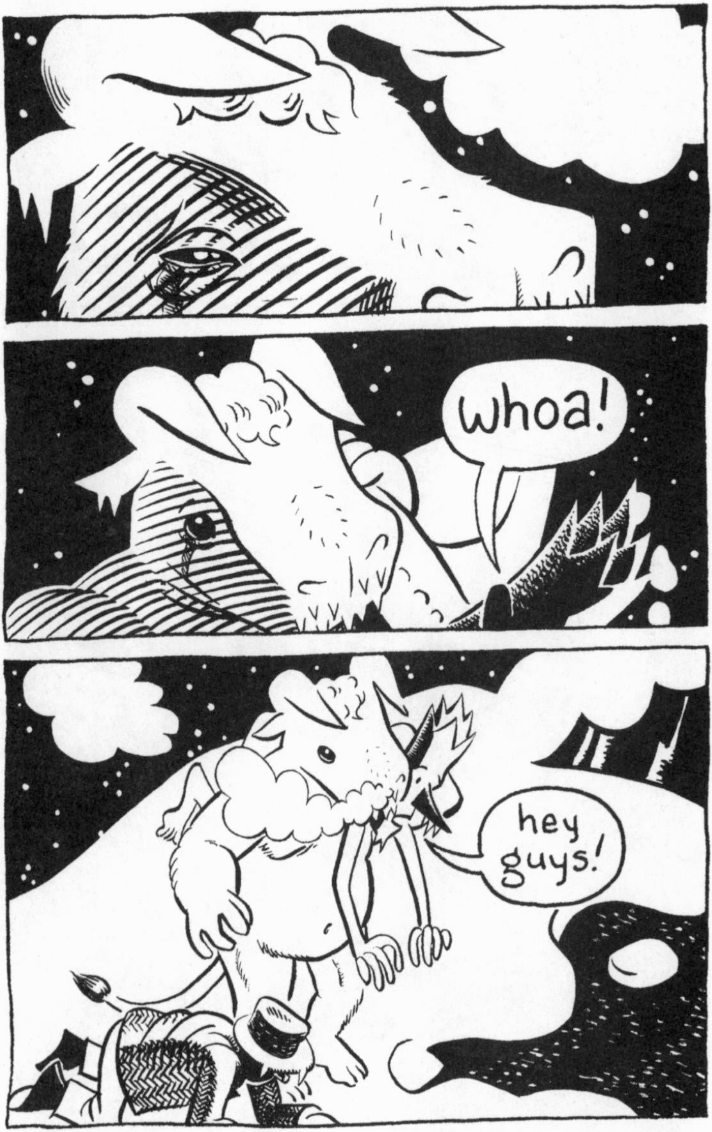
whoa!
hey guys!

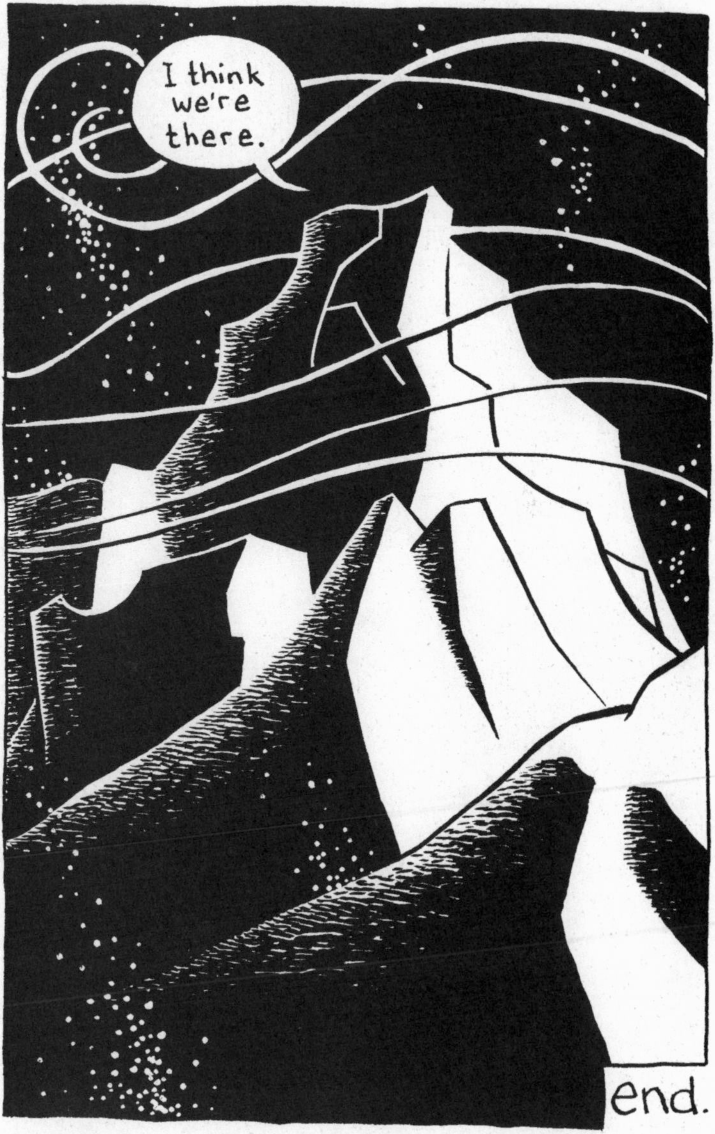
I think we're there.

end.

rowbot, bull, delaware thistle, & the old man on the mountain

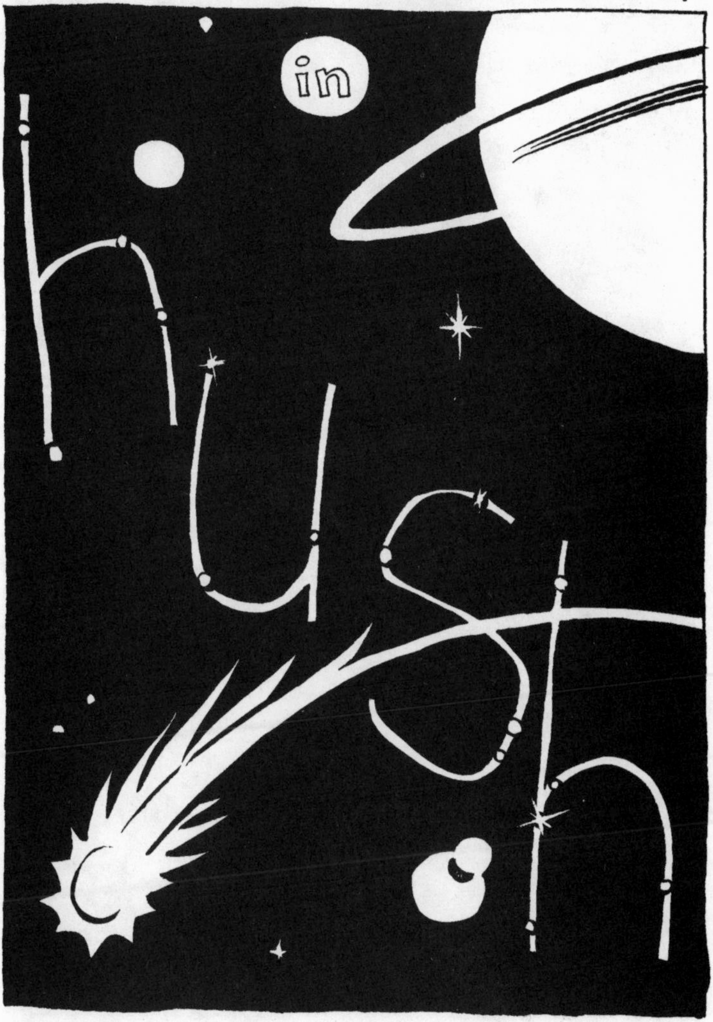
in
hush

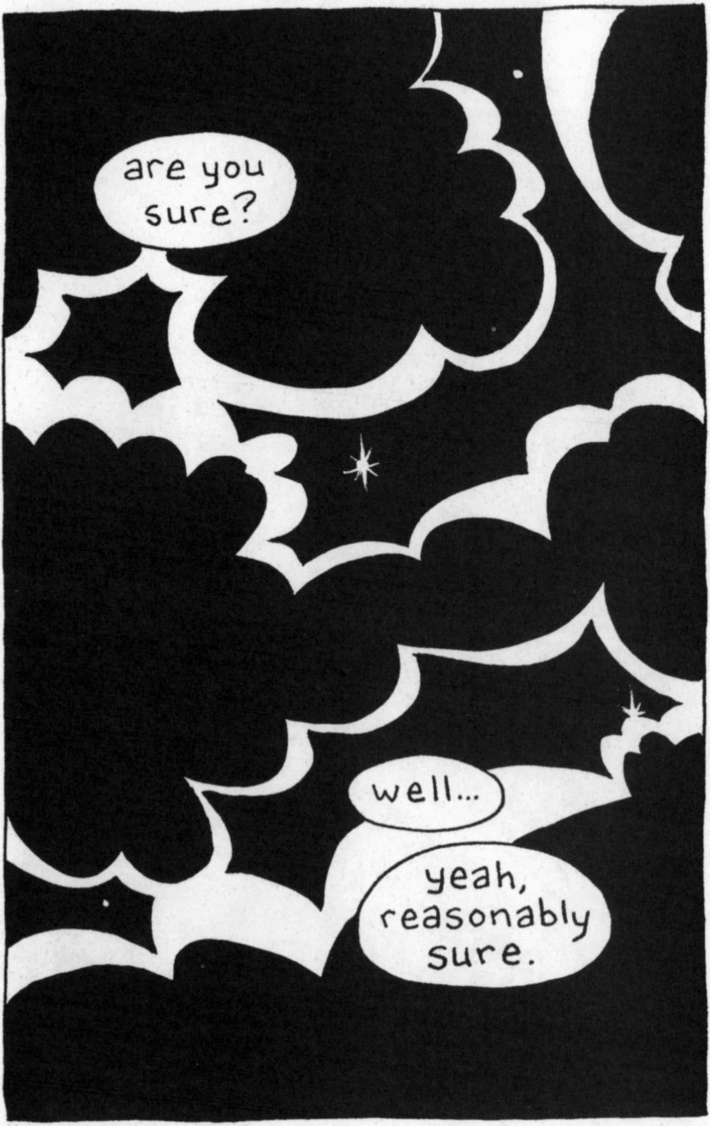
are you sure?
well...
yeah, reasonably sure.

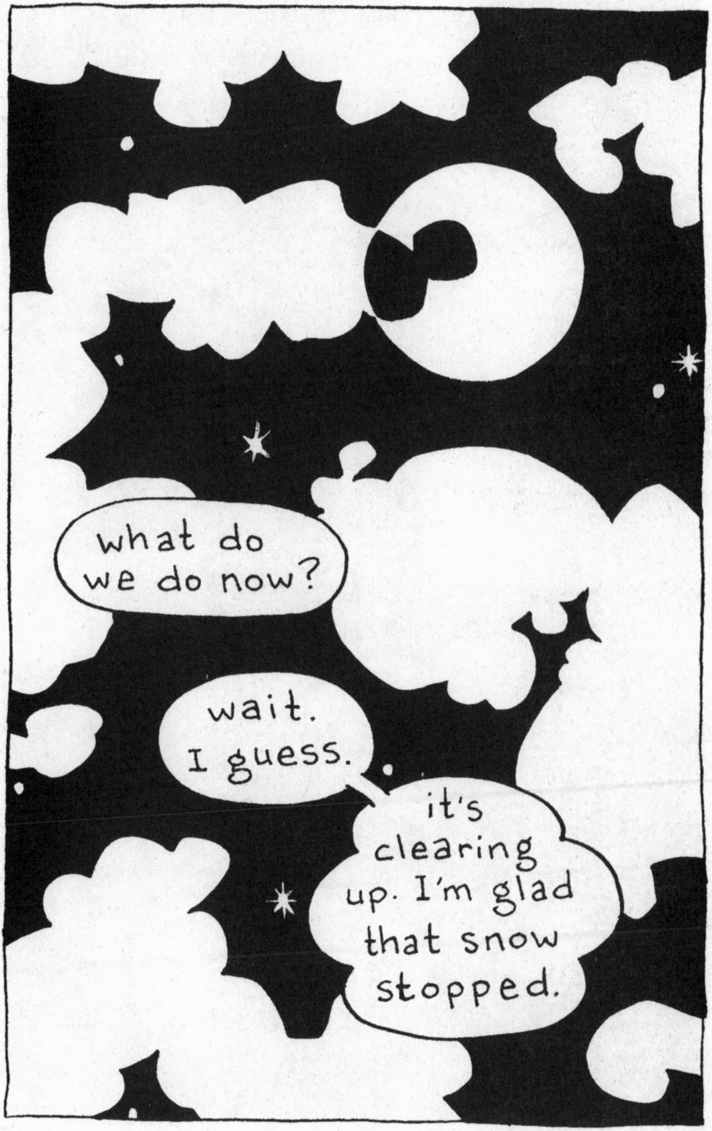
what do we do now?
wait. I guess.
it's clearing up. I'm glad that snow stopped.

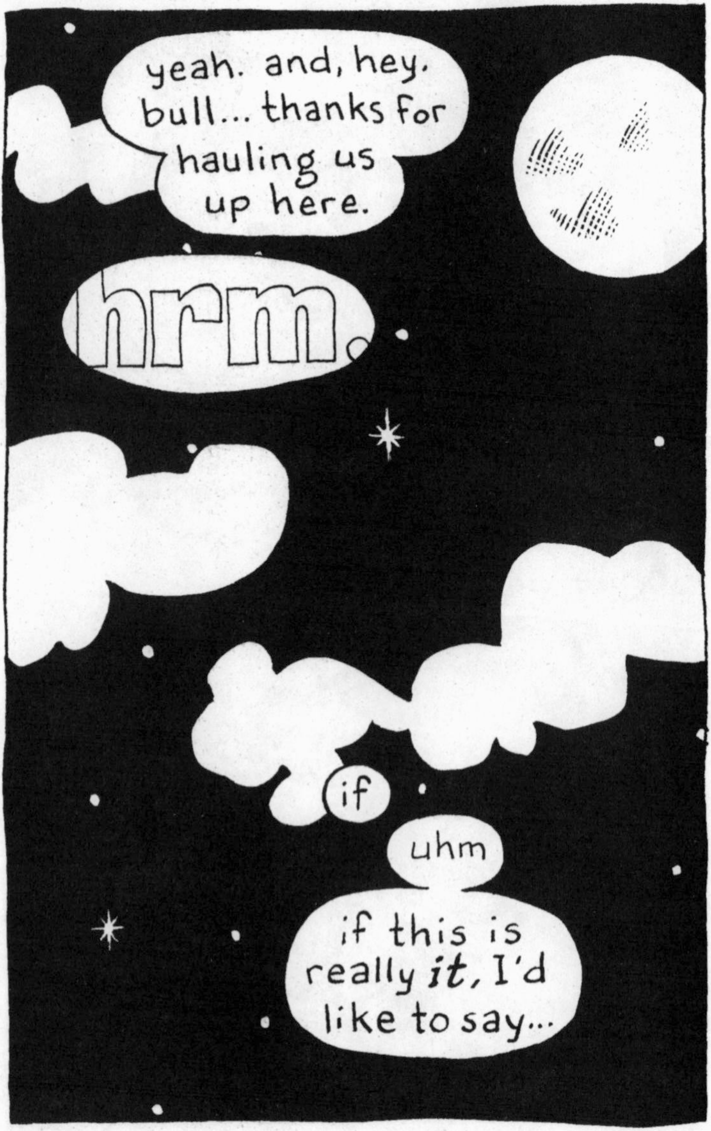
yeah. and, hey. bull... thanks for hauling us up here.
hrm.
if
uhm
if this is really *it*, I'd like to say...

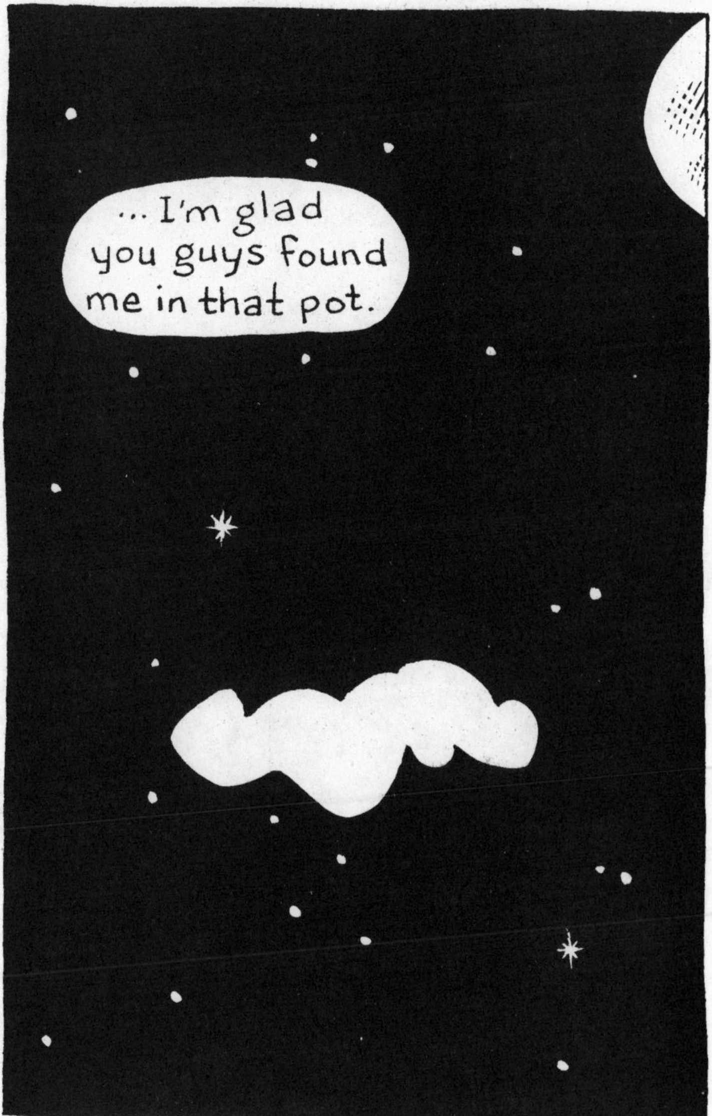
... I'm glad you guys found me in that pot.

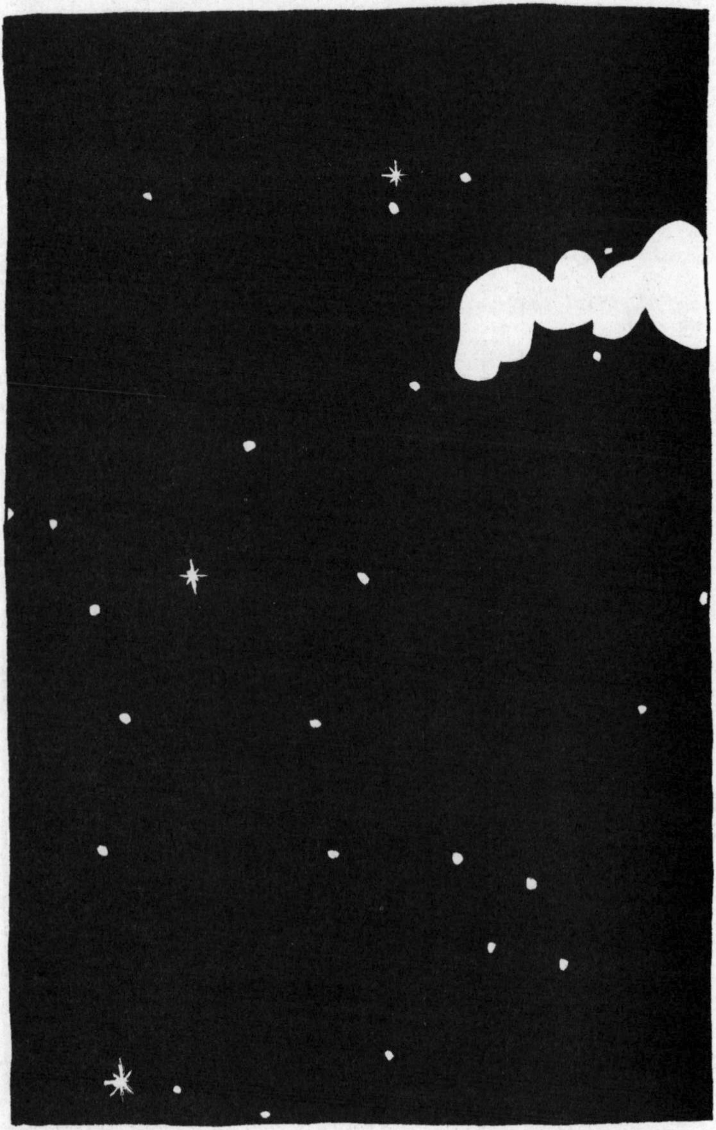

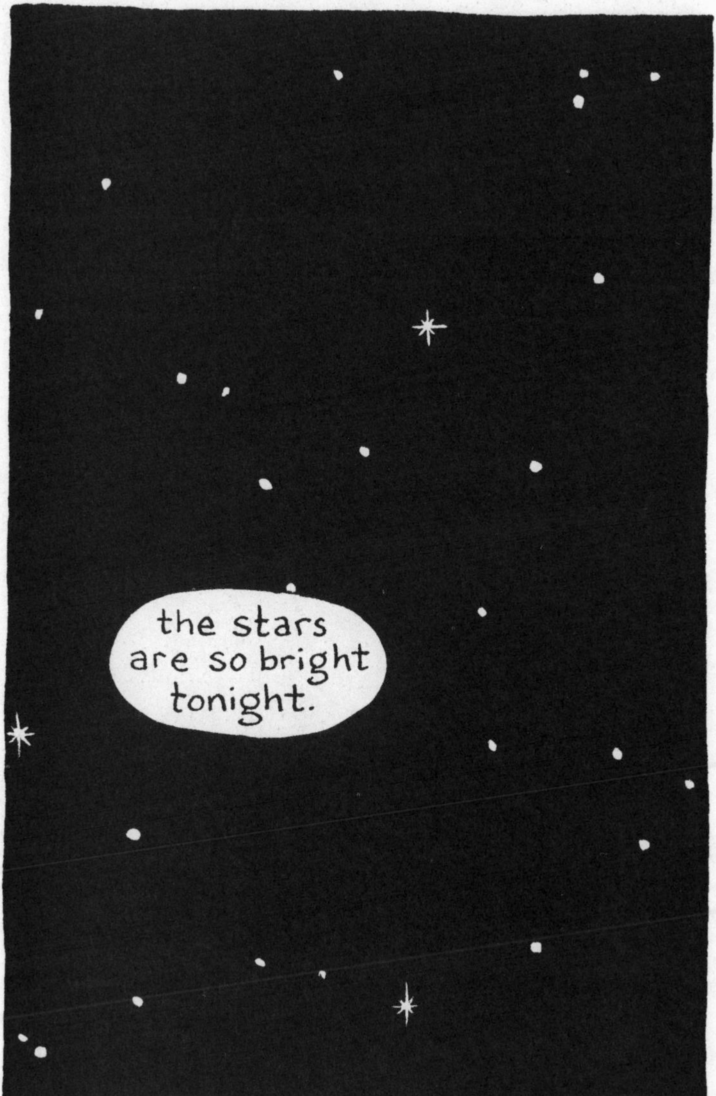
the stars are so bright tonight.

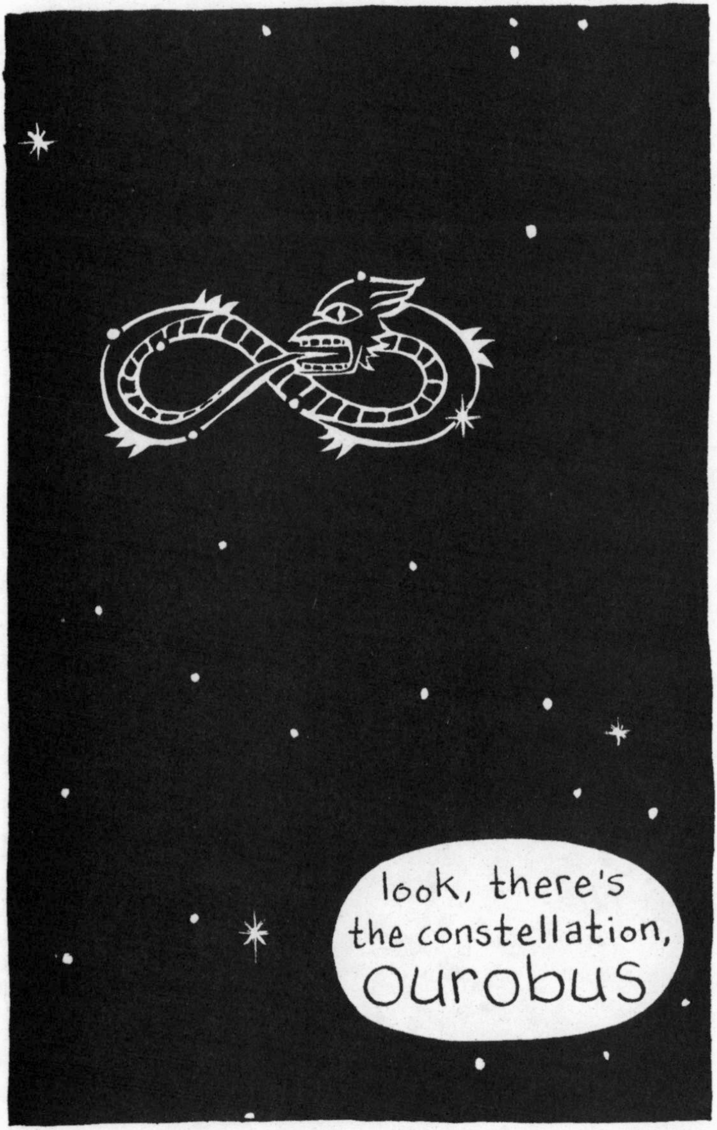
look, there's the constellation, ourobus

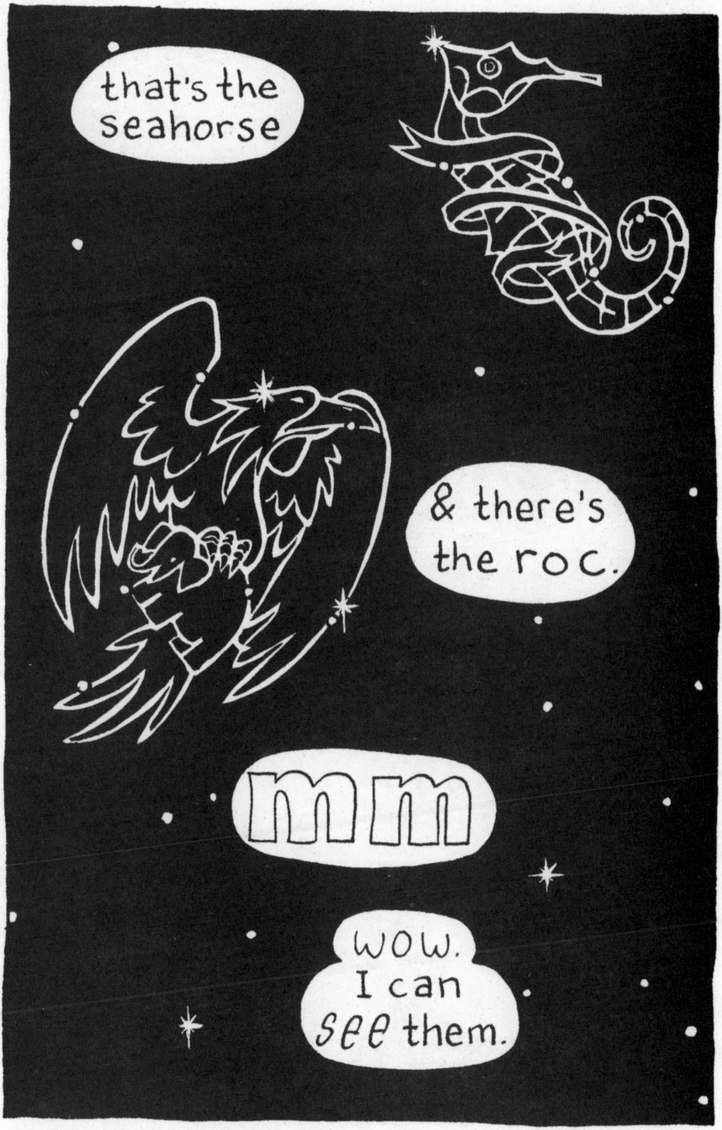
that's the seahorse
& there's the roc.
mm
wow. I can *see* them.

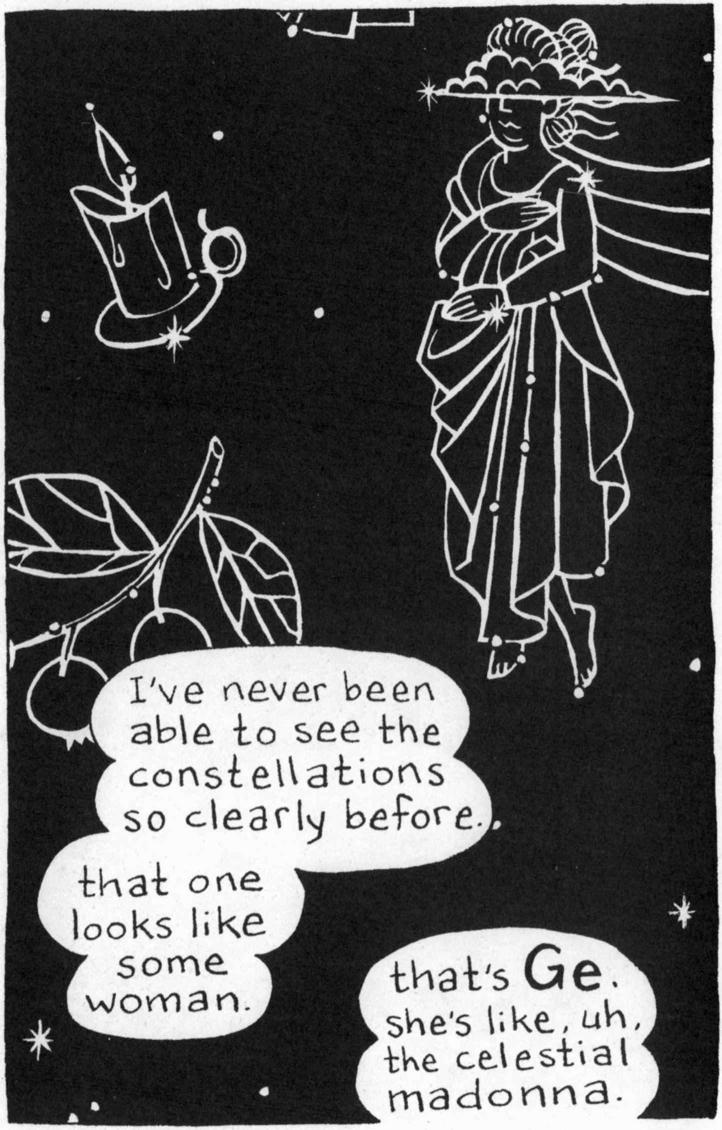
I've never been able to see the constellations so clearly before.
that one looks like some woman.
that's Ge. she's like, uh, the celestial madonna.

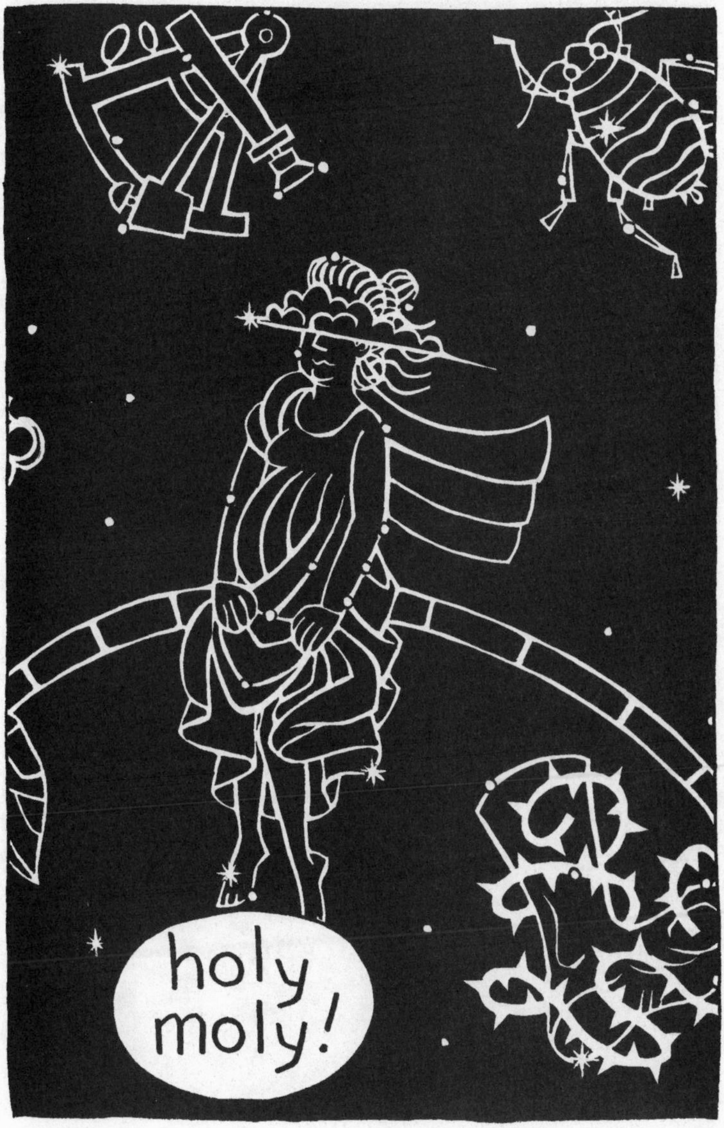
holy moly!

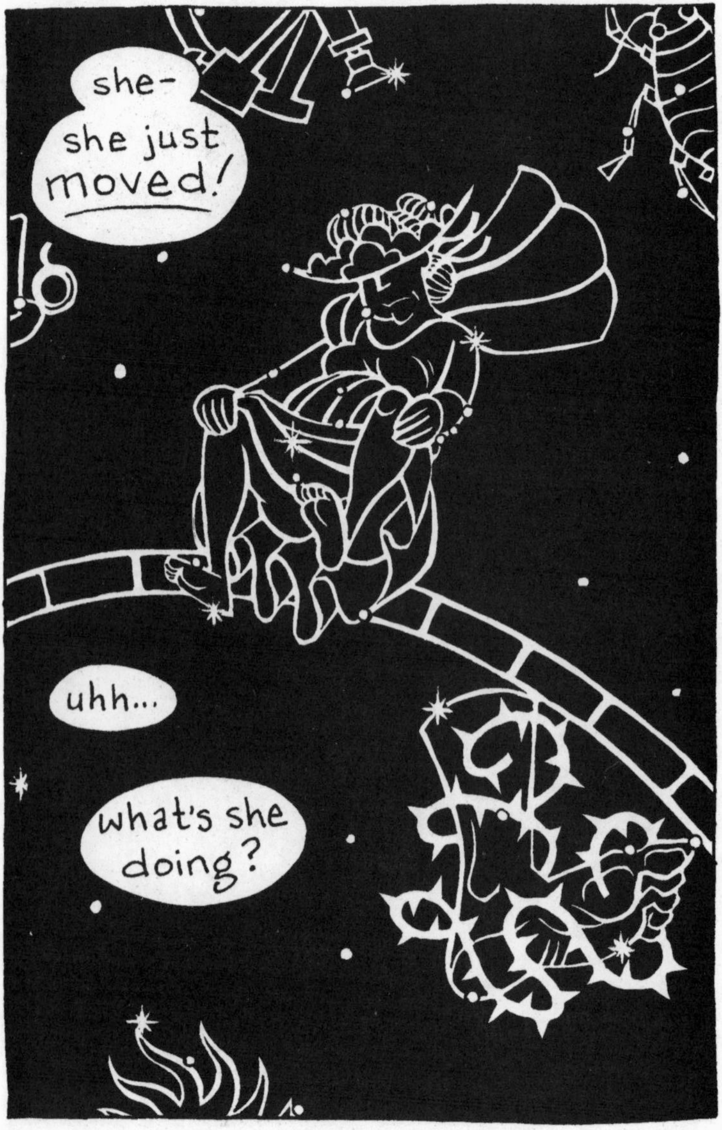
she-
she just moved!
uhh...
what's she doing?

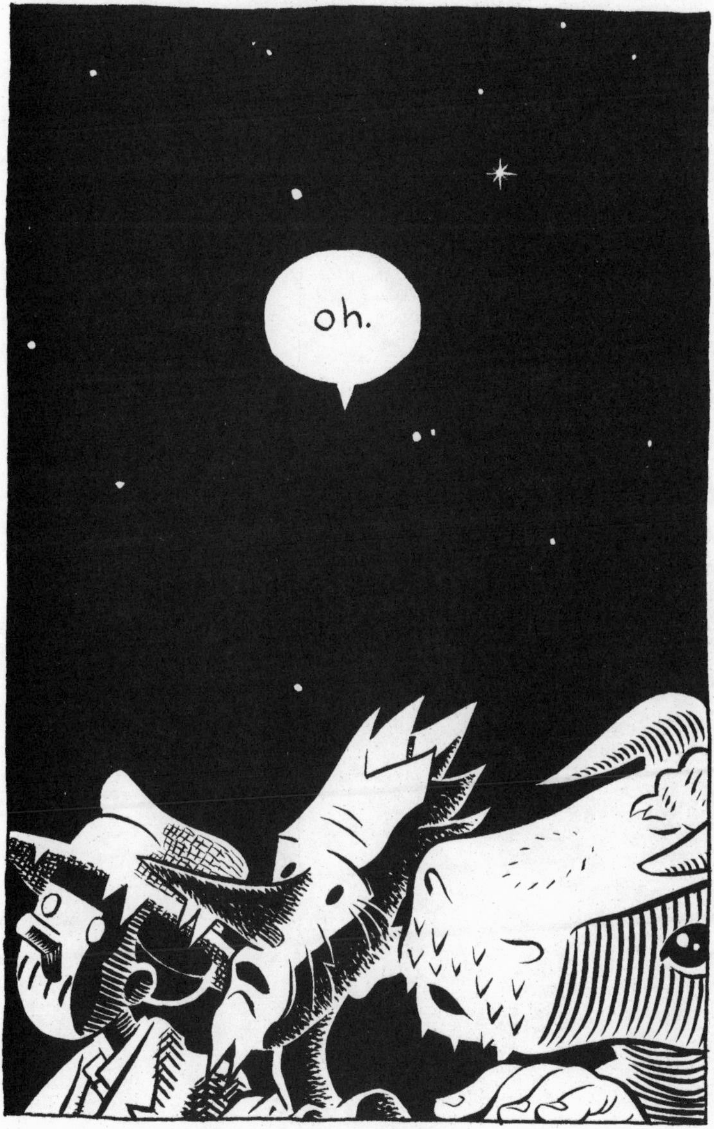
oh.

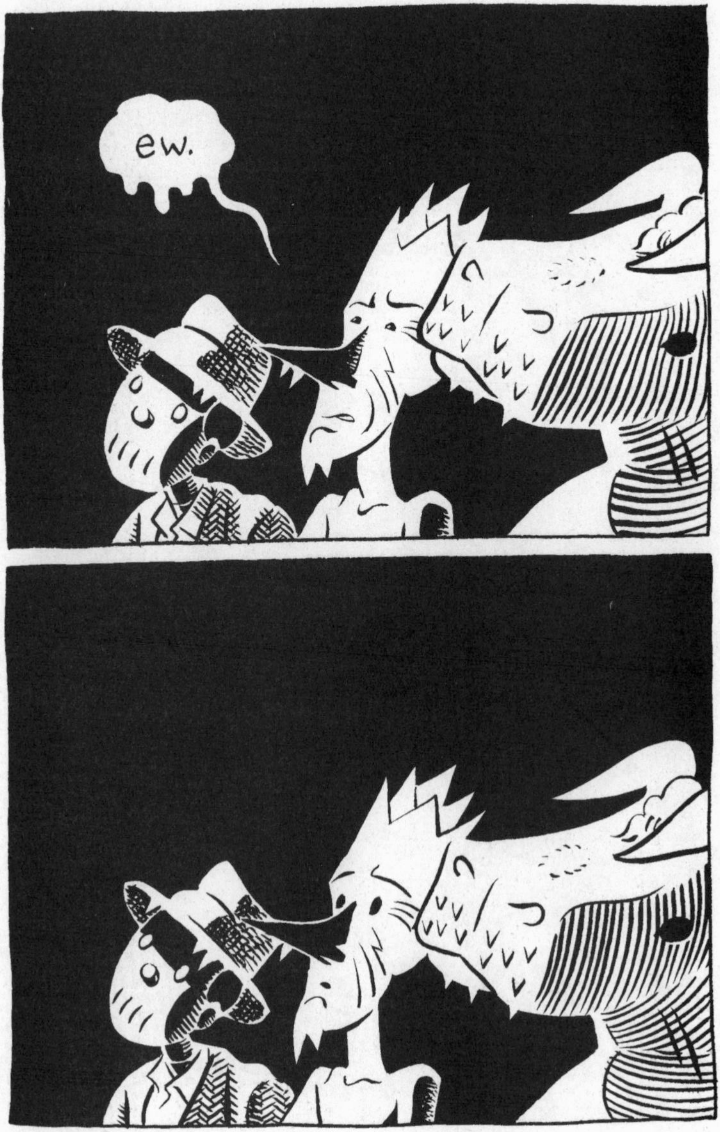
ew.

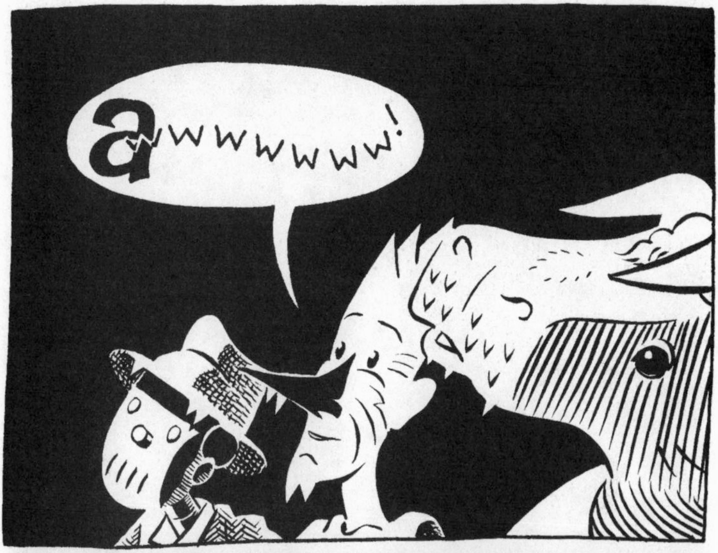
awwwwwww!

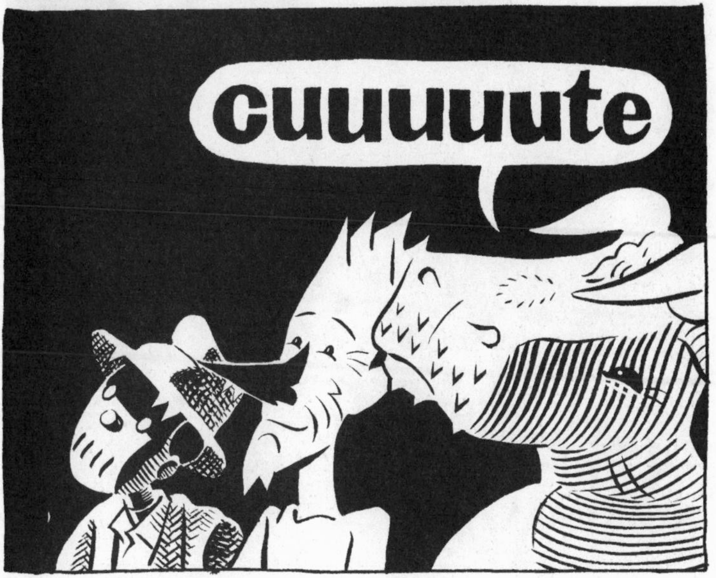
cuuuute

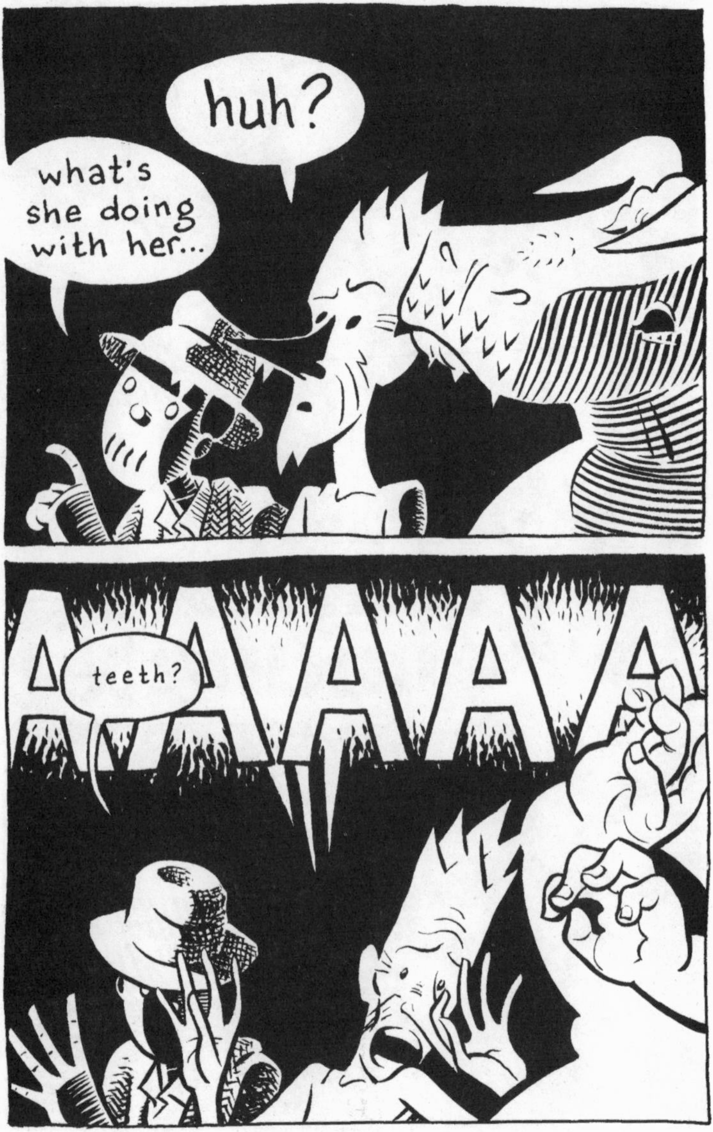
what's she doing with her...
huh?
AAAAA
teeth?

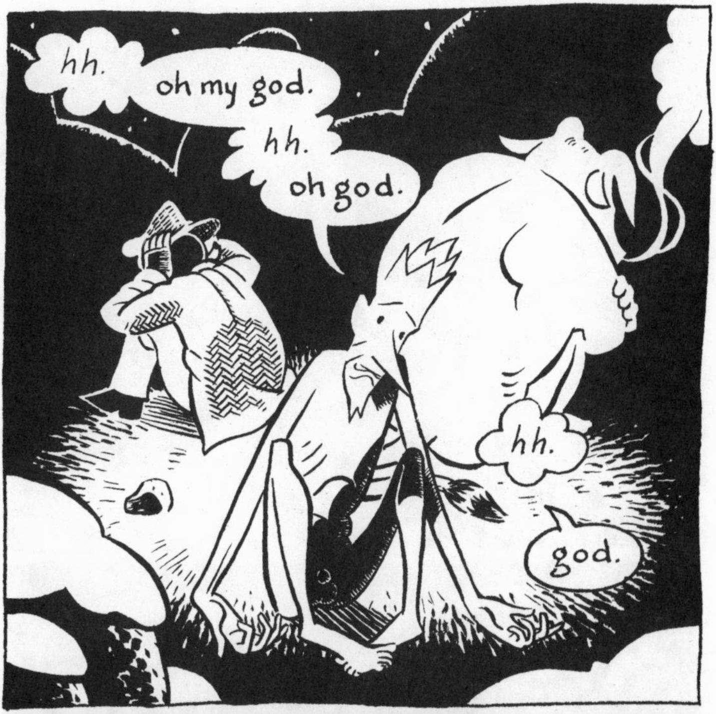
hh.
oh my god.
hh.
oh god.
hh.
god.

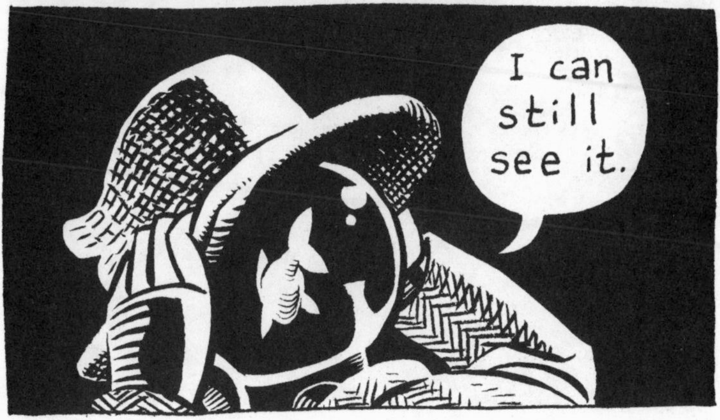
I can still see it.

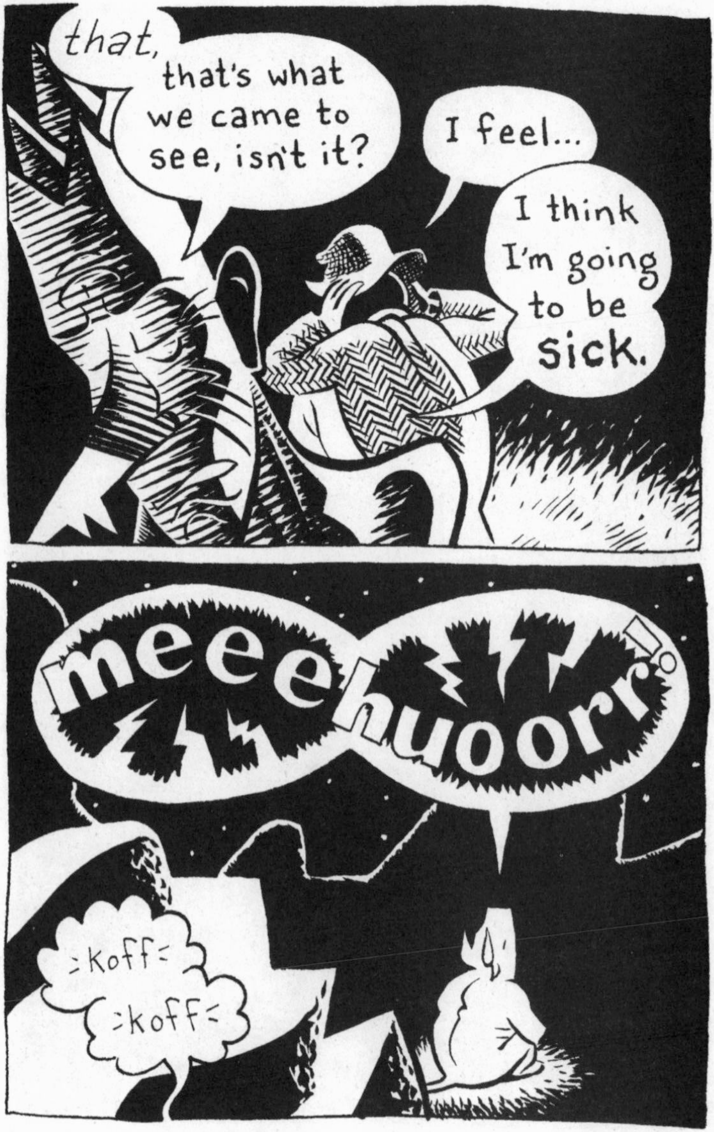
that, that's what we came to see, isn't it?
I feel...
I think I'm going to be sick.
meeehuoorr!
:koff:
:koff:

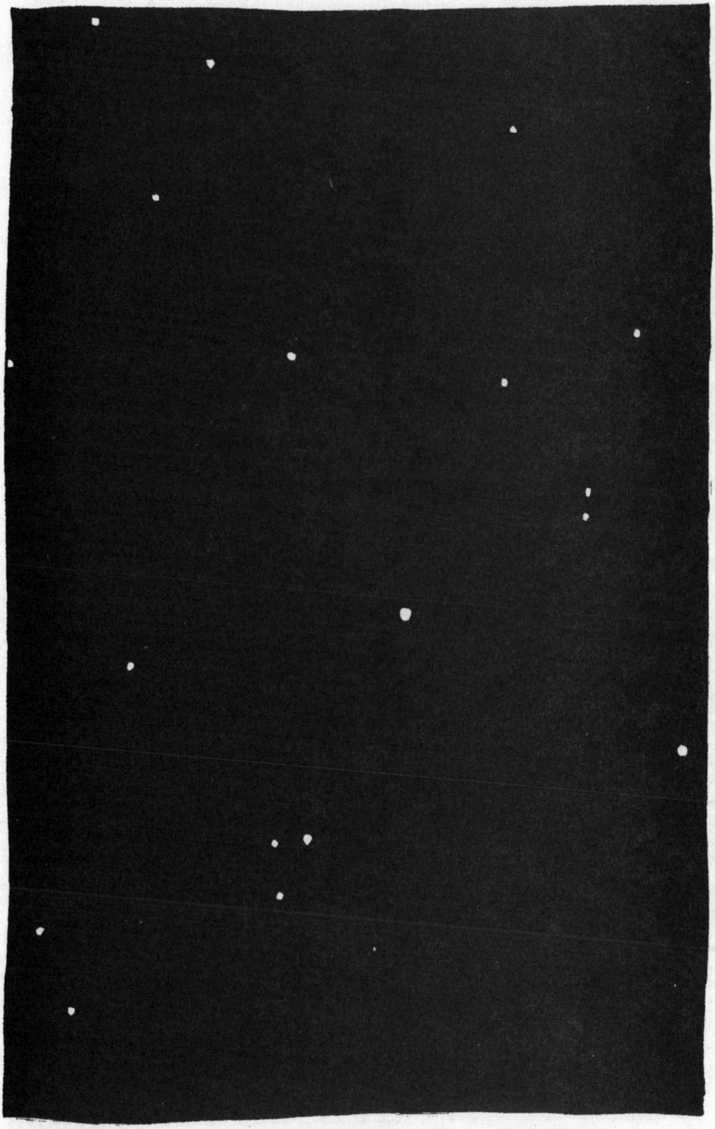

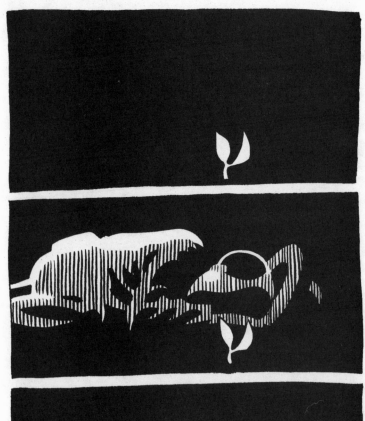

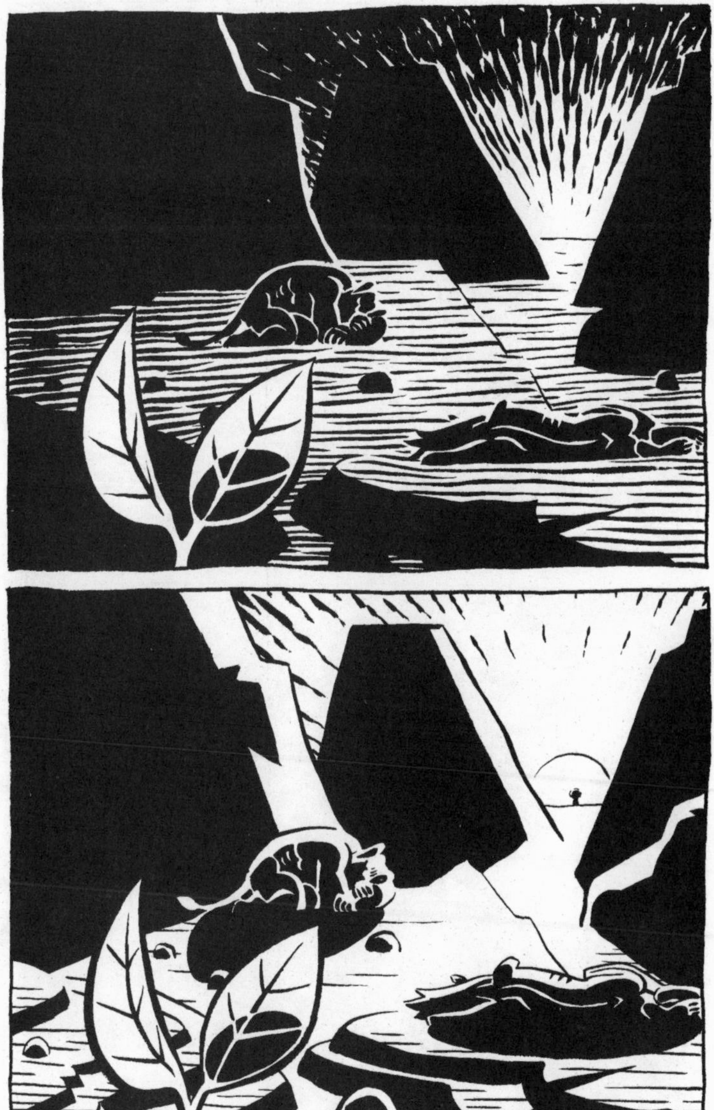

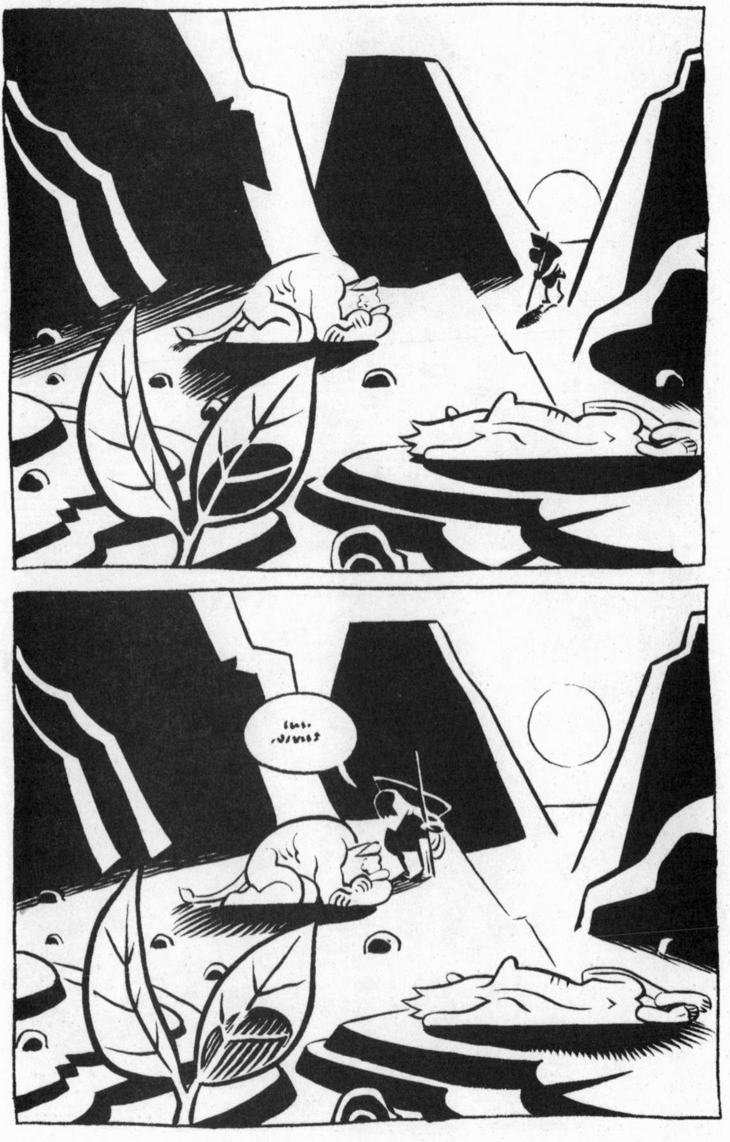

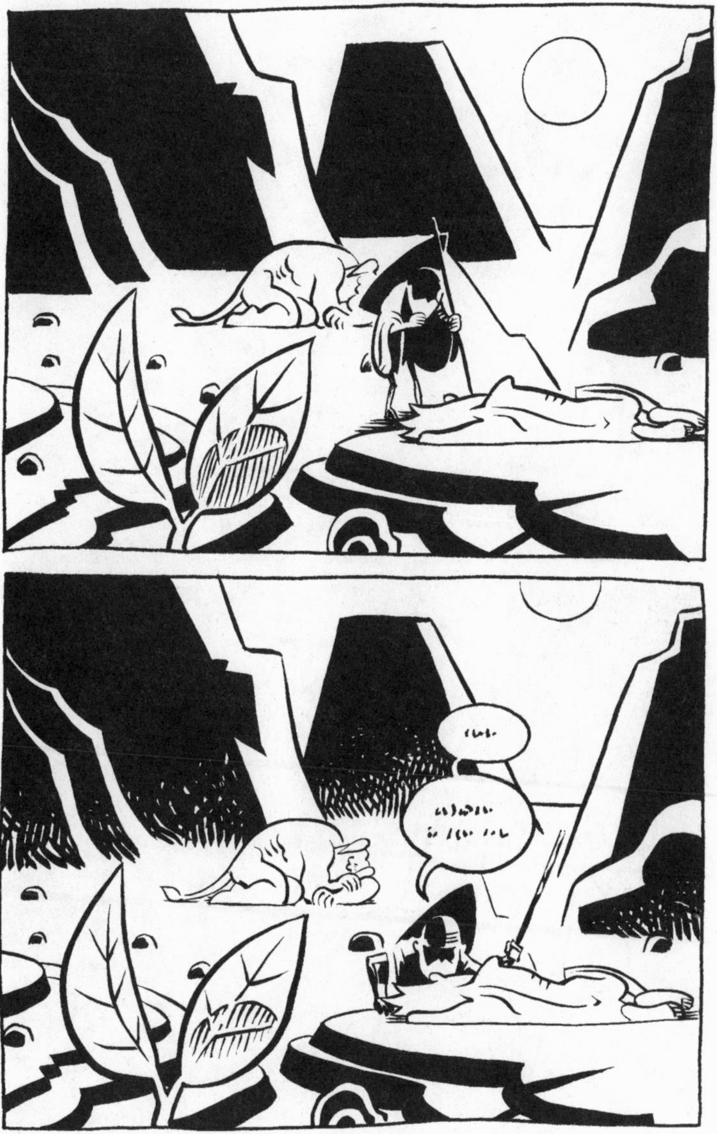

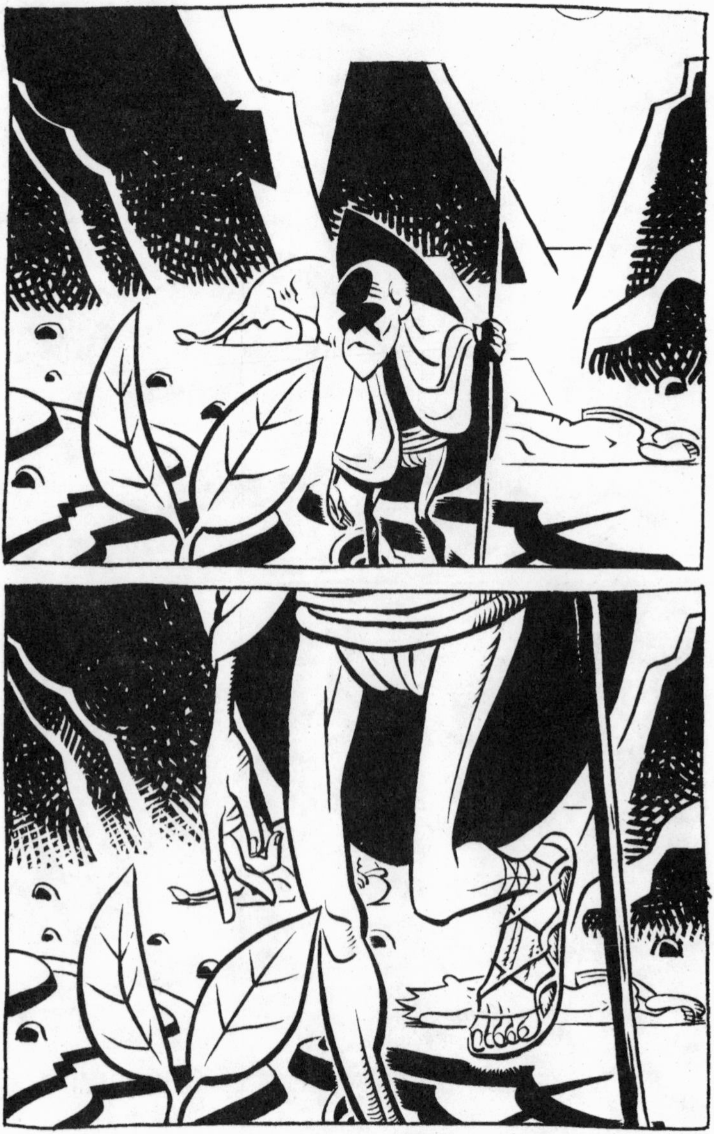

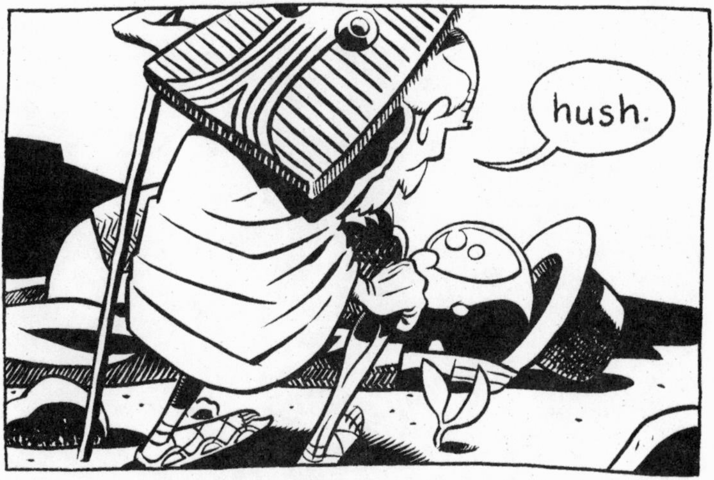
hush.

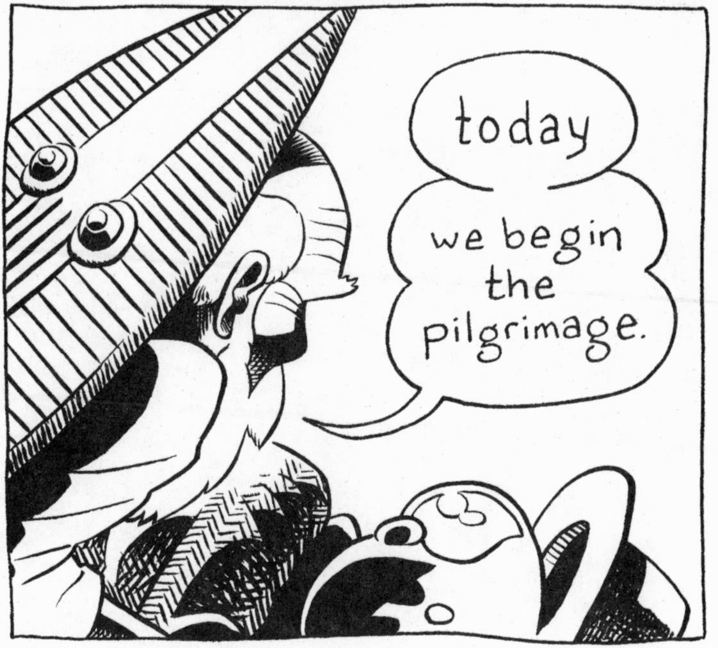
today
we begin the pilgrimage.

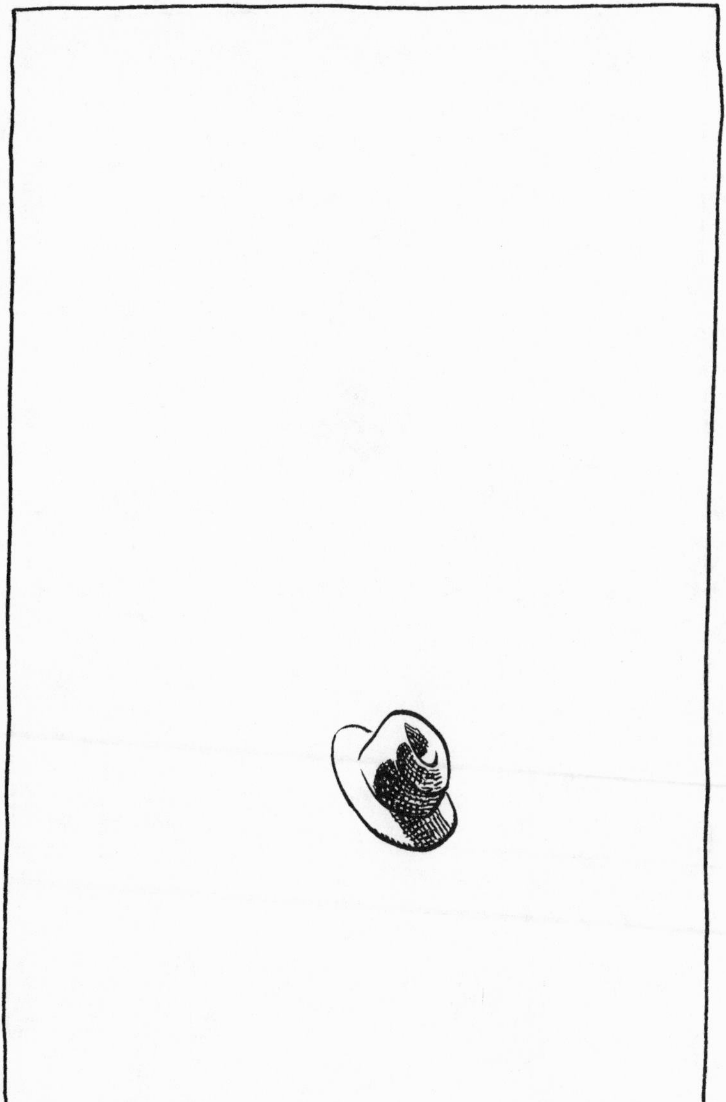

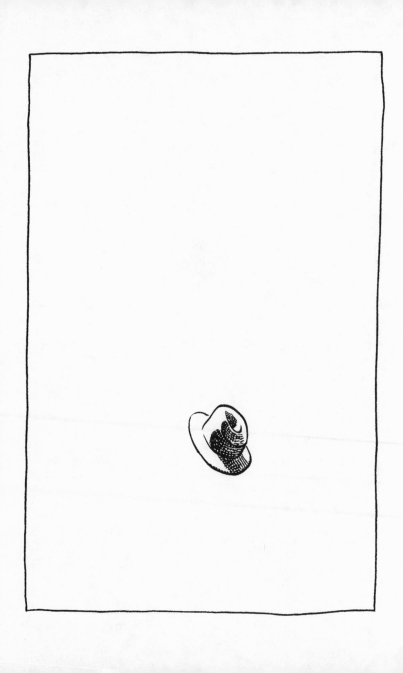

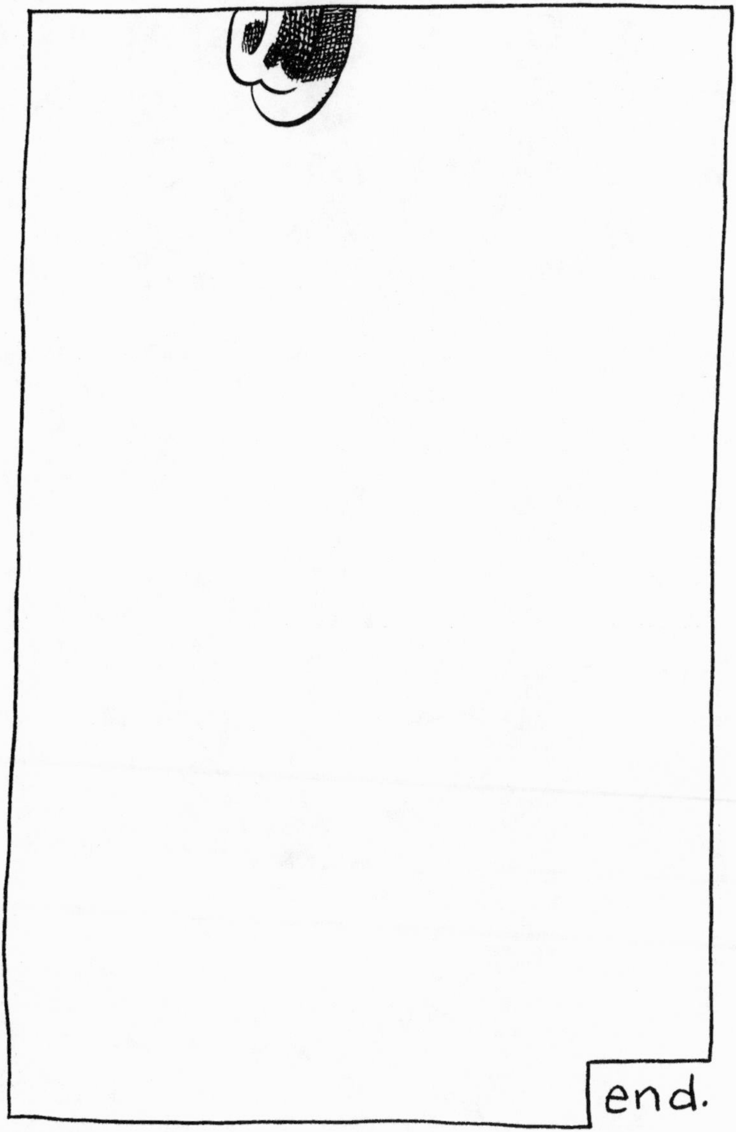

end.

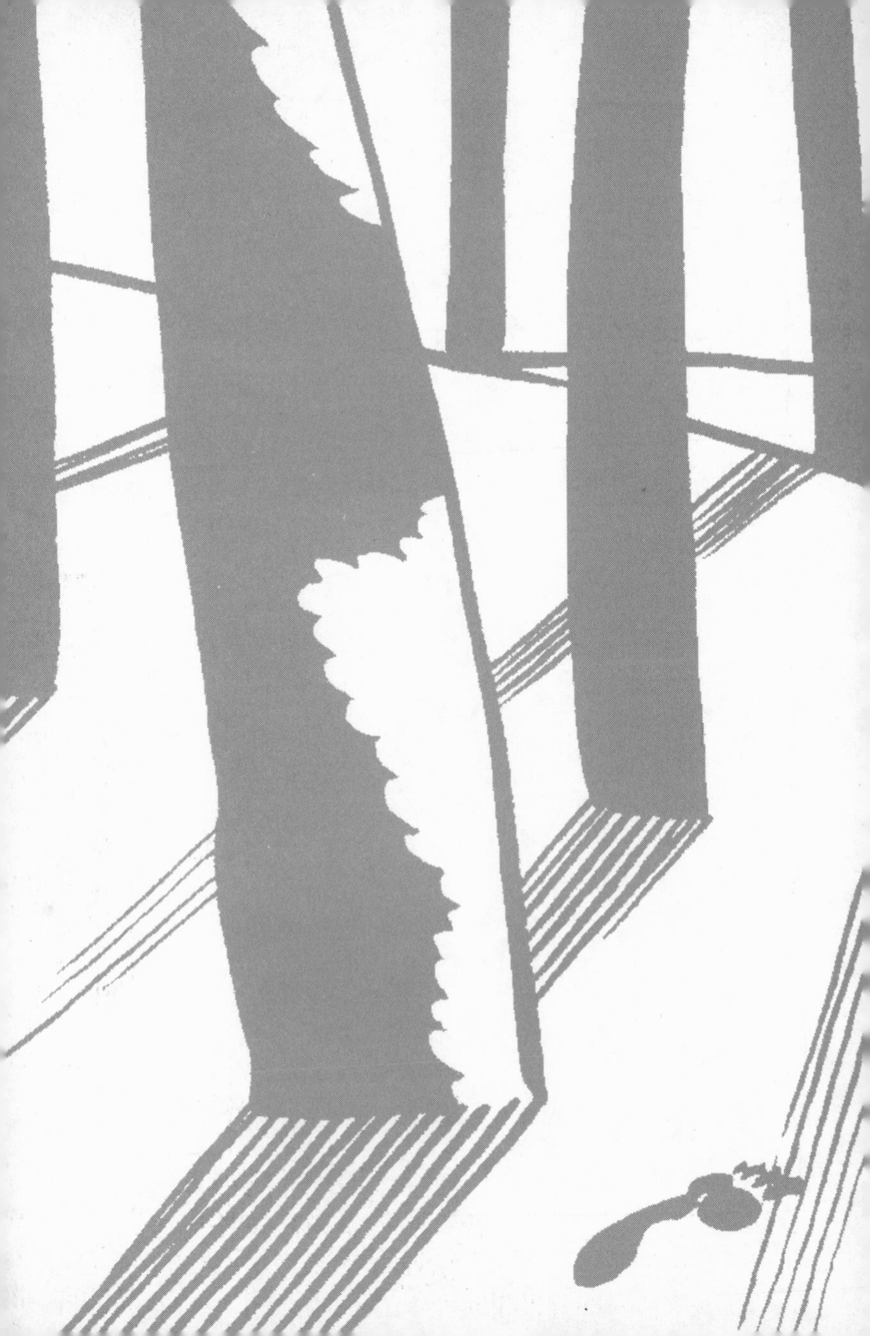